Concise Handbook of
Literary and Rhetorical Terms

Concise Handbook of

Literary and Rhetorical Terms

Michael S. Mills

 Estep-Nichols Publishing

for my son, Jackson

Published in the United States by Estep-Nichols Publishing.

http://www.LiteraryHandbook.com

First Edition

Mills, Michael S.

    Concise Handbook of Literary and Rhetorical Terms/Michael S. Mills

Includes bibliographical references and index.

ISBN: 978-0615271361 (pbk. : alk. paper)

1. Figures of speech   2. English language—Rhetoric

PE1445.A2L3   2010

428.1

Printed in the United States of America.

Acknowledgements

I want to thank the Benton High School English department for their suggestions, ideas, and inspiration in developing this guide. In particular, I want to thank Lisa Pemberton, a veteran teacher of language and literature, who has given me several lenses through which to see and use the terms contained in this book. She is a teacher who continually inspires her students and gives them multiple opportunities to develop as critical readers, and I hope this guide can be a worthwhile reference for her and teachers like her.

I also want to express immense gratitude to my mentor and friend Martha Matthews, who has taught language and literature for over thirty years. My expectation for an editor was to have a person who has devoted her life to teaching the art of analyzing literature and language and who has a keen eye for detail. I instantly thought of Martha. She has given generations of students a clear, compelling vision of how language and literature shapes the world and their own lives, and I am honored to have her experiences help shape this guide.

Finally, I have been blessed by love and patience from my wife, Michelle, as I have worked on this project. She has been steadfast in her support and her enthusiasm, and I cannot state enough my love and appreciation for her.

Preface

The purpose of this handbook is to be a comprehensive, yet accessible, handbook of literary terms that engages the reader on a scholarly as well as practical level. As a literature teacher, my most immediate needs for a literary terms dictionary include concise explanations of the terms I am searching for, accurate pronunciations of the terms, and plenty of pertinent examples to illustrate each concept. Sadly, I could find no one resource that did all of this for me. In the course of compiling this handbook, many respected sources were consulted, but none could offer me a comprehensive list of important literary and rhetorical terms as well as the resources I needed to make use of the terms that were included. Rather, I have had to rely on dozens of resources to find what I am looking for, so I decided to compile a handbook that gave me and my students a comprehensive, accessible, and practical reference under one cover.

This handbook provides

- clear and concise meanings for over 1600 terms, complete with a detailed index

- pronunciations for over 700 terms

- categories grouped by themes, so that related terms are easier to find (and connect to)

- relevant examples, where needed, to illustrate terms in a more practical and conceptual way

- indices that list every literary work and author used in the examples

- the inclusion of terms that have become a part of the literary analysis lexicon only recently, like *blog, eggcorn, found poem, mondegreen, retronym, snowclone,* and *steampunk*

- terms every teacher and student of literature should know but can't find hardly anywhere else, terms like *Négritude, Occam's Razor, schadenfreude,* and *treppenwitz*

Great pains were taken to organize this book in the most logical way possible, but I readily acknowledge that the inherent vagueness among some categories may warrant debate as to the placement of a particular term.

This handbook is, in no way, intended to completely replace the many varied guides and dictionaries that are specialized and cover their entries in more depth. These are all very good references (as such, I have included them at the end of this book in the list of references). I encourage you to consult them as your specialized needs dictate.

In addition, feel free to visit the website **LiteraryHandbook.com** for more ideas and resources.

Table of Contents

academic drama

the practice, which started during the Renaissance, of performing ancient Roman dramas in schools

also referred to as a **school drama**

allegory

(AL uh gore ee)

a narrative that has underlying symbolic meanings; from "speaking otherwise" (Greek)

Examples:

> *Animal Farm* (George Orwell)
> *The Divine Comedy* (Dante)
> *The Pilgrim's Progress* (John Bunyan)
> *The Crucible* (Arthur Miller)

[*see also* beast fable, parable]

anthem

(AN them)

a lyric dedicated to a group, nationality, or movement; from "response" (Greek)

a modern interpretation also includes rock songs that have become so popular that they are used for major events

Examples:

> "The Star Spangled Banner" (Francis Scott Key)
> "The King Shall Rejoice" (George Handel)
> examples of the latter definition include the rock band Queen's "We are the Champions" and "We Will Rock You"

anthology

(an THAHL uh jee)

a collection of poetry or prose, sometimes divided into categories; from "collection of flowers" (Greek)

anti-masque

(AN tee mask)

a type of burlesque or farce that precedes or serves as an interlude for a masque; spelled **antemasque** if preceding a masque

apocalyptic literature

(uh POK uh lip tik)

prose or poetry that includes prophecies of doom and destruction for mankind; from "disclosure" (Greek)

also referred to as **eschatological literature** (ess kuh toh LAHJ ih kull)

Examples:

> *Revelation to John* (Holy Bible)
> "The Second Coming" (William Butler Yeats)
> *The Four-Gated City* (Doris Lessing)

[*see also* dystopia]

---

apocryphal

(uh POK kruh full)

writings of uncertain or unknown authorship or dubious authenticity; the term usually refers to the collection of spiritual writings known as the *Apocrypha*, which are not considered part of the canon (officially recognized books) commonly known as the Holy Bible

---

apology

a work written to defend a person's ideas or to clarify an issue; from "defense" (Greek)

Example:

> Plato's *Apology of Socrates*, which features Socrates defending himself before the governing body of Athens

---

autobiography

an account of one's own life often presented in a continuous narrative; from "self life-writing" (Greek)

[*see also* memoir]

---

beast fable

an allegorical story in which the principal characters are animals; often employs anthropomorphism, a form of personification

also referred to as an **apologue**, **beast epic**, or **bestiary**

Examples:

> "The Nun's Priest's Tale" (Chaucer)
> "Tortoise and the Hare" (Aesop)
> *Animal Farm* (George Orwell)

belles-lettres (bell LEH truh)	generally refers to light nonfiction regarded more for its style than for its substance; from "fine letters" (French) a writer of belles-lettres is a **belletrist** (bell LEH trist) notable belletrists include Max Beerbohm and Aldous Huxley
bildungsroman (BILL doongz roh mahn)	a "coming of age" story; a story that follows the physical, emotional, and spiritual growth of the protagonist; from "novel of formation" (German) also referred to as **erziehungsroman** or **apprenticeship novel** **Examples:** Examples from the 19th century include Charlotte Bronte's *Jane Eyre* and Charles Dickens's *David Copperfield*. In popular culture, the characters Harry Potter (*Harry Potter and the Sorcerer's Stone*, J.K. Rowling) and Luke Skywalker (*Star Wars: A New Hope*, 1977) are both featured in bildungsroman stories—the epics that tell their stories detail their innocence, their growth into a hero role, and the realization of their respective powers. [*see also* Künstlerroman, rite of passage]
biography	an account of a person's life written by someone else; from "life writing" (Greek)
black comedy	a form of literature (usually drama) that treats serious subjects with disillusionment, cynicism, and, often, mocking, sardonic humor also referred to as **black humor** **Examples:** *The Merchant of Venice* (Shakespeare) *Slaughterhouse Five* (Kurt Vonnegut) *Catch-22* (Joseph Heller)
boulevard drama	19th century French domestic comedies primarily intended for commercial development

burlesque

(burr LESK)

a type of parody meant to ridicule a serious work by not treating the subject seriously or by treating an insignificant subject with pomposity and grand style

a burlesque has also acquired an additional meaning as a stage production that includes a striptease or some other sexual performance; from "to ridicule" (Italian)

Examples:

> *The Rape of the Lock* (Alexander Pope)
>
> the rendition of "Pyramus and Thisbe" within *A Midsummer Night's Dream* (Shakespeare)

[*see also* mock epic, travesty]

canon

(KAN un)

a body of writings established as authentic

Example:

> The books that make up the Holy Bible of the Christian church are a canonized text.

[*see also* apocryphal]

caper

a story or subplot that features the progress of a crime from the criminal's perspective

Examples:

> *The Great Train Robbery* (Michael Crichton)
>
> "The Ransom of Red Chief" (O. Henry)

chanson de geste

(shahn sawn deh ZHEST)

Medieval French epic poetry focusing on the lives and romantic adventures of noblemen

divided into a stanza pattern called a **laisse** (LESS *or* LACE)

Example:

> *The Song of Roland* (Anonymous)

[*see also* courtly love, epic]

chapbook

popular ballads, stories, poetry, and other forms of literature published in pamphlet or small book form and sold by peddlers known as chapmen from the 16th to 18th centuries

chivalric romance

(shih VAL rik roh MANTS)

popular romance literature during the Middle Ages depicting adventures and fantastical situations within the scope of an idealized code known as courtly love

also referred to as **medieval romance**

[*see also* courtly love, romance]

chrestomathy

(kress TOM ih thee)

an anthology made up of passages used in the study of language; from "useful learning" (Greek)

chronicle

(KRAHN ih kull)

an accounting of events in chronological order, usually composed as they happen; may come in the form of diaries or narratives

Examples:

> *The Anglo-Saxon Chronicle* (Anonymous)
> *The Diary of Anne Frank* (Anne Frank)

chronique scandaleuse

(kron EEK skahn duh LEWZ)

literature focusing on intrigue, gossip, and scandal in the affairs of royalty and its courtiers

closet drama

a play intended to be read rather than be performed, or a play intended to be performed but never was

Examples:

> *Samson Agonistes* (John Milton)
> *Prometheus Unbound* (Percy Shelley)

comedy

a literary work (usually a play) that does not have the seriousness of a drama; often has a happy ending

Examples:

> *A Midsummer Night's Dream* (Shakespeare)
> *Much Ado about Nothing* (Shakespeare)

comedy of errors
a humorous drama that features a series of complex events, mistaken identities, and, often, significant misunderstandings

Examples:

The Comedy of Errors (Shakespeare)
Much Ado about Nothing (Shakespeare)

comedy of manners
a humorous drama that highlights middle and upper class social codes, particularly with an expression of wit and sophistication

Examples:

Much Ado about Nothing (Shakespeare)
The Importance of Being Earnest (Oscar Wilde)
An Ideal Husband (Oscar Wilde)

[*see also* high comedy]

comparison-contrast essay
an analytical essay that examines the similarities and differences between two or more subjects

confessional literature
works that include the author's or his persona's subjective experiences, which serve to expose very personal feelings and attitudes

conte

(KAWNT)

an allegorical, usually witty, short story featuring elements of fantasy; from "tale" (French)

the **conte philosophique**, from "philosophical novel" (French), is a subgenre and was invented by the French writer Voltaire and is usually a didactic story

Examples:

Gulliver's Travels (Jonathan Swift)
Candide (Voltaire)

coronach

(KOR uh nuhk *or* KAHR uh nuhk)

a Scottish or Celtic lamentation for the dead; a dirge

courtesy book

a book of verse from the late Middle Ages that instructed courtiers on matters of protocol and etiquette

Examples:

Il Libro del Cortegiano (Baldesar Castiglione)

The Compleat Gentleman (Henry Peacham)

---

cyberpunk

(SAHY burr punk)

science fiction involving dystopic futuristic societies in which technology has a major role in plot and character development

Examples:

Bladerunner (1982)

The Matrix (1999)

Neuromancer (William Gibson)

THX-1138 (1971)

---

descriptive essay

an essay that describes, in great detail, some person, place, or thing and relies on abundant details, rich language, and immersive imagery

---

didactic literature

(dahy DAK tik)

poetry and prose meant to be instructive, to teach a lesson

parables and **fables** are common types of didactic literature

Examples:

Aesop's fables

"The Pardoner's Tale" (Chaucer)

---

dime novel

late 19th century American novels focusing on individualistic freedom and adventure; often set in frontier and Civil War times

the term originated from the fact that the novels often cost a dime

[*see also* penny dreadful]

dirge

(DURJ)

a lyrical poem or song of **lamentation** (grief and sadness); from "direction" (Latin)

Example:

> A dirge is specifically mentioned in the following example from the anonymous Old English epic *Beowulf*:
>> Then the Storm-Geat nation constructed for Beowulf
>> a stronghold on the headland, so high and broad
>> that seafarers might see it from afar.
>> That beacon to that battle-reckless man
>> they made in ten days.....
>> Then the warriors rode around the barrow,
>> twelve of them in all, athelings' sons.
>> They recited a **dirge** to declare their grief,
>> spoke of the man, mourned their King.

[*see also* monody, threnody]

---

dithyramb

(DITH ee ram)

a lyric sung to honor Dionysus (Bacchus), the god of wine and merriment; can also describe a wildly impassioned presentation

also referred to as a **rhapsody**

---

domestic tragedy

a tragic play that involves middle class themes

also referred to as a **bourgeois tragedy** (bore ZHWAH)

Examples:

> *A Yorkshire Tragedy* (Thomas Middleton)
> *The London Merchant* (George Lillo)

---

dream allegory

a narrative that relates the contents of a speaker's dream, which contains representations of real life in allegorical form

Examples:

> *The Divine Comedy* (Dante)
> "La belle dame sans merci" (John Keats)
> *Alice's Adventures in Wonderland* (Lewis Carroll)

dystopia

(dis TOPE ee uh)

an anti-utopia; a fictional society dominated by an authoritarian government or some other oppressive environment (e.g., social chaos)

Examples of dystopian works:

> *1984* (George Orwell)
> *Brave New World* (Aldous Huxley)
> *V for Vendetta* (Alan Moore)
> *The Handmaid's Tale* (Margaret Atwood)

écriture féminine

(ey kree TURR fem ih NEHN)

a term coined by feminist Hélène Cixous to denote literary works that convey femininity in their style and tone, as evidenced by a resistance to male-instituted rules and patterns in favor of risk-taking and circularity in writing

elegy

(ELL uh jee)

a formal lyric poem of mourning or solemn reflection

the term **elegiac** (ell uh JAY ik) is used to denote the mood of this type of poem

Examples:

> *In Memoriam* (Alfred, Lord Tennyson)
> *Lycidas* (John Milton)

[*see also* eulogy]

encomium

(en KOH mee um)

a formal expression of praise, particularly a eulogy; from "in celebration" (Greek)

epic	a long, formal narrative poem written in elevated style that recounts the adventures of a hero, who often embodies the traits of a nation or people

also referred to as **epic poetry or heroic poetry**

early epics, particularly transmitted orally, are sometimes referred to as **epos**

epics generally share a wide variety of characteristics:

- the protagonist is a hero of great stature and significance

- the setting is on a grand scale

- the action requires noble and often superhuman actions

- supernatural entities usually involve themselves in the action and affairs of the hero

- written in an elevated style using **heroic verse**, which is unrhymed iambic pentameter in English verse and the dactylic hexameter in Classical Greek and Latin verse

epics generally incorporate certain conventions (known as **epic conventions**):

- invoking of a muse's aid to help in composing the work

- starting the narrative *in medias res*

- introducing the characters in a formal manner (antonomasia)

- using epic similes

Examples:

The Iliad and *The Odyssey* (Homer)
Beowulf (Anonymous)
The Aeneid (Virgil)
Ulysses (James Joyce)

[*see also* chanson de geste, epic hero, epyllion]

---

epistle (eh PIHS ull)	a letter or series of letters regarded as a literary work

epistolary novel

(uh PIHS tuh lair ee)

a narrative in the form of letters or correspondence

Examples:

Dracula (Bram Stoker)

The Screwtape Letters (C.S. Lewis)

---

epitaph

(EPP uh taff)

a commemorative verse meant to be inscribed on a tombstone

Example:

Shakespeare's epitaph:

Good friend, for Jesus' sake forbear,

to dig the dust enclosed here.

Blest be the man that spares these stones,

And curst be he that moves my bones.

---

escape literature

prose fiction that is meant primarily for entertainment but may have some critical literary merit

relies on predictive conventional patterns to satisfy widespread reader expectations

also referred to as **formula literature**

---

essay

a short piece of nonfiction prose that examines a single subject within a limited scope

---

eulogy

(YOO luh jee)

a speech to praise a recently deceased person

[*see also* elegy]

---

exemplum

(ig ZIM plum)

a short narrative used to teach a moral or to assert a religious belief

Examples:

"The Pardoner's Tale" (Chaucer)

[*see also* didactic literature, fable, homily]

---

expository essay

nonfiction prose that is used to explain something, how to make something, how something happened, why people feel the way they do, or what caused an event

fable

a short prose or verse narrative that shares a moral or a practical lesson about life

Examples:

> Aesop's fables
> "The Pardoner's Tale" (Chaucer)
> "The Nun's Priest's Tale" (Chaucer)

[*see also* beast fable, parable]

---

fabliau

(FAB lee oh)

a crude yet humorous tale from the Middle Ages featuring sexual escapades and, often, mockery of the clergy

Examples:

> "The Miller's Tale" (Chaucer)
> "The Reeve's Tale (Chaucer)

---

fantasy

fiction that is, generally speaking, not realistic; includes several genres, including fables, fairy tales, and science fiction

Examples:

> *The Lord of the Rings* (J.R.R. Tolkien)
> "Sleeping Beauty" (Charles Perrault)
> "The Little Mermaid" (Hans Christian Anderson)
> *The Time Machine* (H.G. Wells)

[*see also* incluing, topothesia]

---

farce

a kind of comedy in which ridiculous and often stereotyped characters are involved in far-fetched, silly situations; often, the humor in a farce relies on physical comedy (slapstick); from "stuffing" (Latin)

Examples:

> *The Comedy of Errors* (Shakespeare)
> *The Jew of Malta* (Christopher Marlowe)

[*see also* low comedy, mock epic]

Festschrift

(FEST shrift)

a bound volume of writings by students given as a gift to a teacher or mentor

fiction any writing that features imagined characters and occurrences rather than real ones

fictional nonfiction a term gaining widespread use to describe a literary work that seemingly presents real events and characters but actually is a work of exaggeration or outright imagination

Examples:
> *A Million Little Pieces* (James Frey)
> *When You Are Engulfed in Flames* (David Sedaris)

folktale a story or legend, originating through oral tradition, that has become embedded in a particular region or social group

also referred to as **folklore**

Examples:
> "Babe the Blue Ox"
> "Pecos Bill"
> "Johnny Appleseed"

[*see also* fable, Märchen, tall tale]

gaff refers to cheap, non-elaborate 19th century entertainment, which often included singing, dancing, and tales of adventure

often referred to as **penny gaffs**

gaslight romance a category of supernatural fantasy that is usually set in 19th century England and features iconic literary figures from that era (e.g., G.K. Chesterton, Jack the Ripper, Sherlock Holmes, etc.)

Examples:
> *The Minutes of Lazarus Club* (Tony Pollard)
> *The Waterworks* (E.L. Doctorow)

genre (ZHAHN ruh)	a specific category of literature or film that has certain recognizable elements (conventions) within that category [*see also* subgenre]
ghazal (GAZ ull)	a short lyric poem, usually on the subject of love, which contains couplets with repeated rhymes; a significant form of Arabic poetry also spelled **gazal** or **ghazel** **Example:** *The Ghazals of Ghalib*
Gonzo journalism	generally refers to a type of participant journalism in which the reporter is actively involved in the news being reported; sometimes refers to stream of consciousness nonfiction writing coined by 1960s journalist Hunter S. Thompson to describe his own writings, which include *Fear and Loathing in Las Vegas*; another notable example is Tom Wolfe's *Electric Kool-Aid Acid Test*
Gothic novel (GOTH ik)	a suspenseful story that usually features a gloomy setting and supernatural occurrences **Examples:** *Frankenstein* (Mary Shelley) *Jane Eyre* (Charlotte Bronte) *Wuthering Heights* (Emily Bronte) *Rebecca* (Daphne Du Maurier)
Grand Guignol (grahn gween YALL)	sensational horror literature

graphic novel

a novel presented as a series of illustrated strips or panels

Examples:

Maus: A Survivor's Tale (Art Spiegelman)

Watchmen (Alan Moore)

Sin City (Frank Miller)

[*see also* manga]

hagiography

(hag ee OGG ruh fee)

originally, an idealized religious biography of a saint or martyr; now refers to any biography that idealizes or idolizes the subject of the biography; from "written by inspiration" (Greek)

heroic drama

a tragic drama popularized during the Restoration period

written in heroic couplet form, the heroic drama features a larger-than-life protagonist within the scope of grand themes, characters, and settings

the term was coined by John Dryden with regard to his play *The Conquest of Granada*

high comedy

an intellectual comedy of manners that often includes subtle wit, sarcasm, and irony

Examples:

Pride and Prejudice (Jane Austen)

The Rape of the Lock (Alexander Pope)

historical fiction

a fictional story loosely based on historical fact

Examples:

Les Misérables (Victor Hugo)

A Tale of Two Cities (Charles Dickens)

Forrest Gump (Winston Groom)

history play	a play based, either strictly or loosely, on historical fact
	usually refers to the Shakespearean plays based on various British monarchs
	Examples from Shakespeare:
	King John
	Richard II
	Henry IV, Parts 1 & 2
	Henry V
	Henry VI, Parts 1, 2, & 3
	Richard III
	Henry VIII
	also referred to as a **chronicle play**
homily (HAHM uh lee)	a didactic speech or a **sermon**; from "discourse" (Greek)
Horatio Alger (hoh RAY shee oh AL jurr)	a characterization often given to a story that involves a young protagonist rising from poverty to wealth while learning charity, courage, and empathy
	attributed to the author of several popular 19th century novels with this theme; specific examples include *Facing the World* and *Bound to Rise*
	also referred to as a **rags to riches** or **Cinderella story**
horror	a genre of works that are morbid or disturbing, particularly involving the supernatural, and are intended to frighten, shock, or disgust the reader; from "to cause to tremble or shudder" (Latin)
hymn (HIM)	a song sung to honor a deity or, on occasion, an honored individual
idyll (AHYD ull *or* ID ull)	a short work of prose or poetry that depicts a simple, rural scene
	[*see also* pastoral]

juvenilia

(joov uh NILL ee uh)

the works created during an artist's youth

sometimes used in reference to works designed for the young (**juvenile fiction**)

Examples:

Pastorals (Alexander Pope)

Hours of Idleness (George Gordon, Lord Byron)

The Outsiders (S.E. Hinton)

kabuki

(kah BOO kee)

a Japanese dramatic performance featuring elaborate costumes and staging, musical accompaniment, and dancing; from "song, dance, skill" (Japanese)

kitchen-sink drama

plays, mainly of the 1950s, that depict blue-collar (working class) life in a raw, realistic way

Künstlerroman

(KOON sull roh mahn)

a type of narrative that traces the development of an artist either from childhood or from artistic immaturity; from "artist novel" (German)

Examples:

Doktor Faustus (Thomas Mann)

A Portrait of the Artist as a Young Man (James Joyce)

Cat's Eye (Margaret Atwood)

[*see also* bildungsroman]

legend

an unverifiable or unreliable, and often idealized, narrative of a historical figure

Examples:

King Arthur

Robin Hood

[*see also* folktale, saga]

litany

(LIT uh nee)

a prayer recited by the leader of a congregation alternating with the members of the congregation, who repeat a fixed response in unison

Example:

> Lord have mercy on us.
> *Lord have mercy on us.*
> Christ have mercy on us.
> *Christ have mercy on us.*
> Lord have mercy on us.
> *Lord have mercy on us.*
> Christ, hear us.
> *Christ, graciously hear us.*
> God the Father of Heaven, *have mercy on us.*
> God the Son, Redeemer of the world, *have mercy on us.*
> God the Holy Ghost, *have mercy on us.*
> Holy Trinity, one God, *have mercy on us.*
> (Excerpt from the *Litany of Loreto*)

lipogram

(LIP oh gram)

a text that is composed of words that lack one or more letters of the alphabet

Examples:

> *La Disparition* (George Perec)
> *Gadsby* (Ernest Vincent Wright)

[*see also* Oulipo]

liturgical drama

(lih TURR jih kull)

religious drama that extended from church services in Medieval Europe and often included ritual chanted dialogue between the clergy and the congregation; believed to be the origin of secular miracle and mystery plays

low comedy

a dramatic work whose sole purpose is to provoke laughter through crude humor and exaggerated physical gestures (slapstick)

[*see also* farce]

manga

(MANG uh)

a type of Japanese graphic novel featuring dynamic, stylized artwork; from "whimsical pictures" (Japanese)

manifesto

(man ih FESS toh)

a public declaration of a group's or individual's beliefs and doctrines

Märchen

(mare KEN)

a **fairy tale** or folktale that incorporates supernatural or other fantastical elements

Examples:

"Cinderella" (Charles Perrault)

"Hansel and Gretel" (the Brothers Grimm)

"Sleeping Beauty" (Charles Perrault)

[*see also* folktale, legend, tall tale]

masque

(MASK)

a combination of dramatic and lyric poetry intended for courtly entertainment

memoir

(MEM wahr)

a type of autobiography that usually focuses on a single time period or historical event

Example:

Night (Elie Wiesel)

minstrel show

a medieval performance featuring chansons de gestes and the singing of ballads

a performer in a minstrel show is called a **minstrel**

also refers to 19th century American performances featuring the use of blackface and racial stereotypes to mock African-American culture

[*see also* troubadour]

miracle play	religious plays from the Middle Ages that derived from mystery plays and recounted non-biblical accounts of saints, miracles, and the intervention of the Virgin Mary, the mother of Jesus Christ
	the most notable surviving examples are contained in the forty or so French plays of the *Miracles de Notre Dame* from the 14th century

mock epic	a narrative poem that mocks the epic style by elevating an insignificant subject in a lofty way
	Example:
	The Rape of the Lock (Alexander Pope)
	[*see also* mock heroic]

monodrama	a play with only one character
(MAHN oh drah mah)	**Examples:**
	Maud (Alfred, Lord Tennyson)
	Krapp's Last Tape (Samuel Beckett)
	[*see also* monopolylogue]

monody	an ode intended to be spoken by a single speaker; from "alone song" (Greek)
(MAHN uh dee)	**Example:**
	Lycidas (John Milton)

morality play	popular medieval era plays featuring allegories meant to represent man's moral struggle as a Christian
	Example:
	Perhaps the most well-known example of the morality play is *Everyman*, a short morality play from the 15th century, which recounted Man's progression from being a sinner to being saved.

musical

a loose narrative that primarily consists of musical numbers that extend and elaborate the story; often referred to as a **Broadway show**

Examples:

> *Cats*
> *Les Misérables*
> *Wicked*

mystery

a narrative that contains elements initially hidden from the audience but are eventually revealed to complete the plot

mystery play

Medieval plays based on the Bible; often performed on a wagon (called a **pageant**), which served as the mobile stage

myth

an anonymous traditional story, rooted in a particular society, that usually serves to explain the mysteries of nature and a society's beliefs and customs

Examples:

> "Pyramus & Thisbe" (Roman)
> "Echo & Narcissus" (Greek)
> "Ragnarok" (Norse)
> "The Voice, the Flood, and the Turtle" (Native American-Caddo)

narrative

a literary work or speech that tells a story

a **narrative essay** recounts a series of events in story form; keys to effective narrative writing include logical organization and a vivid recounting of a story's events

nō drama

short, tragic plays popular in 15th century Japan that usually have no plot but feature singing and instrumental music

also referred to as **noh drama**

nonfiction	prose based on facts and historical reality; a story or account that is essentially factual
novel	a long fictional prose narrative, much longer than a short story or a novella; often focuses on many events and includes complex, developed characters
novel of manners	a novel that highlights the protocols and customs of upper class society

Examples:

> *Pride and Prejudice* (Jane Austen)
> *Sense and Sensibility* (Jane Austen)
> *Vanity Fair* (William Makepeace Thackeray)

novel of sensibility	a popular style of emotionally charged 18th century European literature focusing on the positive connection between sensibility and one's understanding of the world

also referred to as a **novel of sentiment** or **sentimental novel**

Examples:

> *The Man of Feeling* (Henry Mackenzie)
> *Pamela, or Virtue Rewarded* (Samuel Richardson)
> *La Nouvelle Héloïse* (Jean-Jacques Rousseau)

novella (no VELL uh)	a fictional prose narrative that is longer than a short story but not as long as a novel; tends to focus on a single event; from "novelty" (Italian)
ode	a complex, generally long lyric poem on a serious subject

sometimes referred to as **occasional verse** if composed for a special event

Examples:

> "Ode to the West Wind" (Percy Shelley)
> "Ode on a Grecian Urn" (John Keats)

off-Broadway

theater productions that are not in the mainstream and often contain risqué elements and provocative themes

also referred to as **fringe theater**

opera

(OPP ehr uh *or* OPP ruh)

a dramatic entertainment with text and musical accompaniment, and sometimes dance

[*see also* comic opera, libretto]

opus

(OH puhs)

an artist's or writer's work; from "work" (Greek)

one's masterpiece (the most popular or most highly regarded work) is often referred to as a **magnum opus**; from "great work" (Latin)

oral tradition

a community's cultural and historical traditions passed down by word of mouth and often in narrative form

Examples:

The Iliad, The Odyssey, Beowulf, and the Biblical Gospels began as oral literature.

paean

(PEE un)

a song of praise, victory, or thanksgiving

[*see also* hymn]

panegyric

(pan uh JEE rik)

a lengthy, formal expression of praise

Example:

You all did love him once, not without cause:
What cause withholds you then, to mourn for him?
O judgment! thou art fled to brutish beasts,
And men have lost their reason. Bear with me;
My heart is in the coffin there with Caesar,
And I must pause till it come back to me.
(*Julius Caesar*, III.ii, Shakespeare)

parable

(PAIR uh bull)

a short, allegorical didactic story that conveys a moral belief

parody (PAIR uh dee)	imitation of a literary work or film–or the style used by a writer or filmmaker–in order to ridicule the work and its writer or producer or to have light-hearted fun at the expense of the imitated work

Examples:

> Miguel Cervantes's *Don Quixote* (a parody of medieval knight errant tales)
>
> Sir Walter Raleigh's "The Nymph's Reply to the Shepherd," (a parody of Christopher Marlowe's "The Passionate Shepherd to His Love")

passion play	a play that recounts the New Testament story of the suffering and crucifixion of Jesus Christ originally performed in the 13th century and continues to modern times

pastoral (PASS tore ull)	a type of literature that portrays country life in idyllic, idealized terms; sometimes referred to as **bucolic** or **georgic** literature

Examples:

> *Lycidas* (John Milton)
>
> *The Shepheardes Calendar* (Edmund Spenser)
>
> "The Passionate Shepherd to His Love" (Christopher Marlowe)

penny dreadful	popular but poorly written 19th century British novels or novelettes that focused on adventure, mystery, and crime the term originated from the fact that the novels often cost a penny [*see also* dime novel]

periodical

(peer ee ODD ih kull)

a journal of contemporary issues, ideas, and opinions published at regular intervals

often referred to as a **magazine**

Examples:

Early American examples include *General Magazine*, *Independent Reflector*, and *Pennsylvania Magazine*.

Modern examples include *Time*, *Newsweek*, *Car and Driver*, *Sports Illustrated*, and *Vogue*.

persuasive essay

a composition that is used to convince people to think a certain way or to do something; a key to effective persuasive writing is providing clear reasoning and support for one's positions

picaresque novel

(PIK uh resk)

an episodic narrative focused on a character from the lower class of society on a journey; from "story of a rogue" (Spanish)

the picaresque novel form began with the 16th century Spanish novel *Lazarillo de Tormes*

Examples:

The Adventures of Huckleberry Finn (Mark Twain)

Joseph Andrews (Henry Fielding)

Tom Jones (Henry Fielding)

polemic

(poh LEM ik)

a detailed attack against a person or institution; from "pertaining to war" (Greek)

Examples:

Aeropagitica (John Milton)

"Civil Disobedience" (Henry David Thoreau)

[*see also* invective]

prequel

(PREE kwill)

a literary work that is set before a later, related work (sequel); prequel is a portmanteau of *pre* and *sequel*

a prequel can be written before or after the sequel

Examples:

> J.R.R. Tolkien's *The Hobbit*, published in 1937, is a prequel to *The Lord of the Rings* trilogy, published in 1954.
>
> Jean Rhys's *The Wide Sargasso Sea*, published in 1966, is a prequel to Charlotte Bronte's *Jane Eyre*, published in 1847.

problem play

a drama that focuses on a social problem and (sometimes) offers a solution

also referred to as a **thesis play**

Examples:

> *A Doll's House* (Henrik Ibsen)
> *The Crucible* (Arthur Miller)

prothalamion

(proh thah LAM ee on)

lyric verse in honor of a wedding

also referred to as **epithalamium** (EPP ih thuh LAY mee um)

psalm

(SAWLM)

a sacred hymn or song; notably, one from the Holy Bible

psychological novel

a novel that focuses on a character's thoughts, feelings, and spirituality rather than on a specific plot or the setting; a **character analysis** of sorts

pulp fiction

a derogatory term for magazines of the 1920s and 1930s containing risqué short stories and excerpts from novels

the American **detective novel** began as pulp literature

regional novel

a work whose story rests largely on a richly detailed region or locale and its inhabitants

[*see also* local color, vernacular]

revenge tragedy

popular particularly in the Elizabethan period, these plays centered on the theme of revenge; also referred to as a **tragedy of blood**

Examples:

The Spanish Tragedy (Thomas Kyd)

Hamlet (Shakespeare)

revue

(reh VYOO)

a variety show featuring singing and dancing

roman à clef

(roh MAH nuh KLAY)

a novel that describes real life events masked as a work of fiction; from "novel with a key" (French)

Examples:

The Sun Also Rises (Ernest Hemingway)

Postcards from the Edge (Carrie Fisher)

Primary Colors (Joe Klein)

The Devil Wears Prada (Laura Weisberger)

roman à these

(roh mah nuh TAYZ)

a novel with a message of social importance; from "thesis novel" (French)

Example:

Uncle Tom's Cabin (Harriet Beecher Stowe)

roman-fleuve (roh MAHN FLURV)	a series of novels that feature the continuing adventures of a character or set of characters; from "river novel" (French)

Examples:

> *The Lord of the Rings* trilogy (*Fellowship of the Ring, The Two Towers, Return of the King*) (J.R.R. Tolkien)
>
> Harry Potter series (*Harry Potter and the Sorcerer's Stone, Harry Potter and the Chamber of Secrets, Harry Potter and the Prisoner of Azkaban, Harry Potter and the Goblet of Fire, Harry Potter and the Order of the Phoenix, Harry Potter and the Half-Blood Prince, Harry Potter and the Deathly Hallows*) (J.K. Rowling)
>
> Jason Bourne series (*The Bourne Identity, The Bourne Supremacy, The Bourne Ultimatum* (Robert Ludlum); *The Bourne Legacy, The Bourne Betrayal, The Bourne Sanction, The Bourne Deception* (Eric Van Lustbader))
>
> *Twilight* series (*Twilight, New Moon, Eclipse, Breaking Dawn*) (Stephenie Meyer)

[*see also* prequel, sequel, serial, trilogy]

romance	a fictional adventure story with idealized characters and fantastical settings

romantic comedy	light-hearted play that features young lovers, misunderstandings, and, eventually, a happy ending

Examples:

> *A Midsummer Night's Dream* (Shakespeare)
>
> *Much Ado about Nothing* (Shakespeare)

saga (SAH gah)	a lengthy narrative or legend, particularly one of Icelandic or Norse origin, that recounts heroic adventures also refers to lengthy narratives that chronicle a dynasty or generations of interrelated characters; from "saying" (Norse)

Examples:

> *Sturlunga Saga*
>
> *Egils Saga* (Snorri Sturluson)

[*see also* epic, legend]

satire (sah TIRE)	using wit, sarcasm, or humor, a work that mocks or critiques a person or an element of society; from "medley" (Latin)
	satire that is particularly coarse or mean-spirited is known as a **lampoon**
	classic satire includes the following:
	Juvenalian (joo vuh NEY lee un)—serious, often harsh, satire with a determined moral purpose (e.g., Jonathan Swift's *A Modest Proposal*)
	Horatian (huh RAY shun)—satire aimed at gently mocking the follies of mankind with wry amusement (e.g., Ben Jonson's "On the Famous Voyage")
	Menippean (meh NIP ee un)—satire often preoccupied with the follies of intellectualism and philosophy; also known as **Varronian satire** (e.g., Voltaire's *Candide*)

science fiction	a type of narrative fiction that is based on scientific concepts and explores fantastical possibilities; often referred to as "**sci-fi**"
	Examples: *I, Robot* (Isaac Asimov) "The Cold Equations" (Tom Godwin) *Journey to the Center of the Earth* (Jules Verne)

Senecan tragedy	five-act closet dramas written by the Roman poet Seneca
	these dramas feature ghosts and other supernatural beings as well as a plot filled with violence, revenge, and bombastic rhetoric
	profoundly impacted Renaissance dramas

sentimental comedy	eighteenth-century dramas featuring incredibly virtuous middle class protagonists overcoming moral temptation; these dramas heavily rely on sentimentality rather than on humor
	also referred to as a **drama of sensibility**
	Examples:
	The Funeral: A Comedy (Richard Steele)
	The School for Lovers (William Whitehead)
sequel (SEE kwill)	a literary work that is complete in itself but continues the narrative of a previous work; from "that which follows" (Latin)
	Examples:
	J.K. Rowling's *Harry Potter and the Chamber of Secrets* is a sequel to *Harry Potter and the Sorcerer's Stone*.
	Alexandra Ripley's *Scarlett* is the sequel to Margaret Mitchell's *Gone with the Wind*.
serial	a story that is divided into sections and is published independently
	also refers to radio and television programs that are connected and tell a continuing story
	[*see also* episode, prequel, roman-fleuve, sequel]
shaggy dog story	a type of tall tale that ends anti-climactically or with a pun
	Examples:
	"Shah Guido G." (Isaac Asimov)
short story	a brief fictional prose narrative that includes a plot structure as well as complex characterization

slapstick

a type of physical comedy that often uses exaggerated physical gestures and comic violence

Examples:

> Early movies featuring Charlie Chaplin, Buster Keaton, and the Three Stooges often used slapstick comedy.

[*see also* low comedy]

slave narrative

an autobiography by a freed or escaped slave describing his or her experiences

Example:

> *Narrative of the Life of Frederick Douglass* (Frederick Douglass)

Southern Gothic

a style of writing particular to the American South that features characters who are distressed, disturbed, or delusional and situations that represent a critical view of Southern culture

Examples:

> *Absalom, Absalom!* (William Faulkner)
>
> *Cat on a Hot Tin Roof* (Tennessee Williams)
>
> *To Kill a Mockingbird* (Harper Lee)

speculative fiction

a term coined by writer Robert A. Heinlein to describe literature that portrays characters, settings, or situations in a world never known before or an alternate form of the existing universe

[*see also* cyberpunk, dystopia, science fiction, steampunk, utopia]

steampunk

a type of science fiction writing, popularized in the late 20th century, that weaves elements of modern technology in settings resembling 19th century Victorian England

Examples:

> *The Difference Engine* (William Gibson and Bruce Sterling)
>
> *The League of Extraordinary Gentlemen* (Alan Moore and Kevin O'Neill)
>
> *Morlock Night* (K.W. Jeter)

[*see also* cyberpunk, gaslight romance]

subgenre

(sub ZHAN ruh)

a category within a larger, more general category of literature

a particularly distinct and specialized genre is referred to as a **niche genre** (NICH ZHAN ruh)

[*see also* genre]

tale

a narrative that has the effect of being spoken to the reader

[*see also* narrative, short story]

tall tale

a highly unlikely story; sometimes referred to as a **yarn**

tetralogy

(teh TRAHL oh jee)

a set of four connected literary works meant to be viewed as one complete work as well as four individual works

sometimes referred to as a **quadrilogy**, but this term is nonstandard

Example:

> *Henry VI, part 1*; *Henry VI, part 2*; *Henry VI, part 3*; and *Richard III* (Shakespeare)

[*see also* prequel, sequel, trilogy]

threnody

(THREN uh dee)

a lamentation for the dead; from "wailing song" (Greek)

Example:

> *In Memoriam* (Alfred, Lord Tennyson)

[*see also* dirge, elegy, monody]

tragedy

a serious drama focusing on a character who endures personal trials and undergoes unexpected reversals of fortune; from "goat song" (Greek)

Examples:

> *Antigone* (Sophocles)
> *Oedipus the King* (Sophocles)
> *Macbeth* (Shakespeare)
> *Romeo and Juliet* (Shakespeare)

tragicomedy

unlike a tragedy in its conventional sense, this play usually includes moments of lightheartedness and ends with a happy ending; later tragicomedies also included elements of **poetic justice**

Example:

> *The Merchant of Venice* (Shakespeare)

[*see also* black comedy]

travesty

(TRAV uh stee)

the trivialization of a serious subject as a parody; from "dressed in disguise" (Latin)

Example:

> The lighthearted and buffoonish treatment of the tragedy of Pyramus and Thisbe in Shakespeare's *A Midsummer Night's Dream* is a type of travesty.

[*see also* burlesque, mock epic]

treatise

(TREE teez)

a formal, comprehensive analysis of a subject

Examples:

> *Origin of the Species* (Charles Darwin)
> *Das Kapital* (Karl Marx)
> *The Art of War* (Sun Tzu)

trilogy (TRILL uh jee)	a set of three connected literary works meant to be viewed as one complete work as well as three individual works **Example:** *The Lord of the Rings* trilogy, which consists of the following parts: *The Fellowship of the Ring*, *The Two Towers*, and *The Return of the King* [*see also* prequel, sequel, tetralogy]

utopia
 	
(yoo TOPE ee uh)
	a perfect world, or so the reader is led to believe; a pun on the Greek words *outopia* (no place) and *eutopia* (good place)
	
	Examples of utopian novels:
	
	    Utopia (Sir Thomas More)
	    Island (Aldous Huxley)
	
	[*see also* dystopia]

vaudeville (VAHD vill)	light entertainment, often used as an interlude also referred to as a **comic opera**
vignette (vin YET)	a particularly well-crafted short story or episode that is self-contained but often a part of a larger work; also refers to an ornamental illustration on a blank page before or after the chapters in a book; from "little vine" (French) **Example:** Sandra Cisneros's novella *The House on Mango Street* is a collection of vignettes that focus on specific moments and episodes in her narrator's life.
whodunnit	a popular term for detective and mystery novels

Literary Periods and Movements

Acmeism (AK mee izm)	refers to early 19th century Russian poets who countered the Symbolist movement by advocating accuracy and precision in writing notable Acmeists include Anna Akhmatova, Nikolai Gumilev, Osip Mandelstam, and Sergei Gorodetsky
Aestheticism and Decadence Movement (ess THET ih sizm / DEK uh dents)	occurred during the latter part of the Victorian Period (1880-1900) much of the literature from this movement included novels and lyric poetry that emphasized brevity and a focus on nonconformity and counter-culturalism the concept of **art for art's sake** (art has inherent value even without a specific purpose) developed throughout this movement, and its chief proponent was Oscar Wilde
Age of Sensibility	refers to the period from 1745-1785 in English literary history much of the literature during this time focused on decorum, empathy, and sensitivity notable writers during this time were Samuel Johnson and Henry Fielding also referred to as the **Age of Johnson** part of the **Age of Enlightenment**, which was also known as the **Age of Reason**
agitprop (AJ it prop)	a term applied to the propaganda movement, respective to dramatic form, that followed the Russian Revolution of 1917 the term is a portmanteau of the words *agitation* and *propaganda*

American Romanticism	the period that spanned from 1820 to 1860 in American literary history
	much of the literature during this time focused on rejecting the notions of the earlier neoclassical movement and embracing nature and passion rather than science and reason; self-awareness was often a major theme during this time
	notable writers during this time were Ralph Waldo Emerson, Nathaniel Hawthorne, Henry David Thoreau, and Walt Whitman
	also referred to as the **American Renaissance**
	[*see also* Dark Romantics, Romantic Period Transcendentalism]
Angry Young Men	refers to authors, playwrights, and, particularly, the anti-heroes of various plays from the mid-20th century in which characters in the work demonstrate defiant, disapproving attitudes toward society
	the term gained widespread use by journalists, particularly to describe Jimmy Porter, the dark, rebellious protagonist in John Osbourne's 1956 play *Look Back in Anger*
art nouveau (ART noo VOH)	an ornate architectural style that heavily influenced the illustration of literature and periodicals of the late 19th century; from "new art" (French)

Augustan Age
(awe GUSS tun)

refers to the restoration of the monarchy and the span of King Charles II's reign in England (1700-1745)

much of the literature during this time focused on restoring the art from the time of Roman poets Ovid and Virgil (during the reign of the emperor Augustus)

the literary focus was on balance, harmony, and elegance

notable writers during this time were Daniel DeFoe, Alexander Pope, and Jonathan Swift

also referred to as the **Age of Pope**

part of the **Age of Enlightenment**, also known as the **Age of Reason**

avant-garde
(AH vahnt gard)

a style of writing that is pioneering, innovative, or advanced for its time

examples include Virginia Woolf's and William Faulkner's use of stream of consciousness and James Joyce's innovations in plot and character development

[*see also* Futurism, Modernism, Postmodernism, Vorticism]

Beat Generation

refers to the American writers who wrote nontraditional and counterculture literature generally during the 1950s

prominent writers during this time include Allen Ginsburg and Jack Kerouac

Bloomsbury group

an influential group of early 20th century writers from the Bloomsbury area of London

prominent members included Clive Bell, Vanessa Bell, E.M. Forster, Roger Fry, John Maynard Keynes, Lytton Strachey, Leonard Woolf, and Virginia Woolf

Caroline Age	refers to the period of Charles I's reign (1625-1649)
	this era was dominated by the works of the Cavalier and Metaphysical poets
	prominent writers during this time were John Milton, John Donne, George Herbert, and Robert Herrick
Cavalier Poets	refers to a group of early 17th century poets who modeled themselves after Ben Jonson and the tenets of Classicism; they abandoned the traditional sonnet form yet still focused on themes of love
	prominent members consisted of Thomas Carew, Robert Herrick, Richard Lovelace, and Sir John Suckling
	also referred to as the **Tribe of Ben** or **Sons of Ben**
Classicism	a literary approach heavily influenced by Greek and Roman literature, particularly with respect to simplicity and reason; markedly contrasted **Romanticism**, which valued passion over reason
	[*see also* Neoclassical Period]
Commonwealth Era	refers to the period of Puritan rule in England (1649-1660)
	much of the literature during this time was sophisticated and political; notably, there was a lack of dramas being published as theaters were closed by order of the Puritan parliament
	prominent writers during this time were John Milton, Thomas Hobbes, Andrew Marvell, and Robert Herrick
	also referred to as the **Puritan Interregnum** (PURE ih tun in turr REG num)
coterie (KOH tuh ree)	a group of friends or writers with similar literary interests

Dadaism

(DAH dah izm)

a literary movement of the early 20th century that challenged traditional norms of art and culture by producing works marked by randomness and nonsense; from "hobby-horse" (French)

notable poets of this short-lived movement included T.S. Eliot and Ezra Pound

[*see also* surrealism]

Dark Romanticism

a movement of the 19th century in America that paralleled the Romantic period

this movement, however, focused more on the darker aspects of humanity and nature rather than the optimism expressed in **Transcendental** thought

themes common in Dark Romantic writing were sin, guilt, and the depravity of man

notable dark romantic writers were Nathaniel Hawthorne, Herman Melville, and Edgar Allan Poe

[*see also* American Romanticism]

dirty realism

a term applied to the work of late 20th century American short story writers who wrote about small town, blue collar themes using simple language and form

notable writers incorporating this style were Raymond Carver, Jayne Anne Philips, and Tobias Wolff

Edwardian Period

refers to the span of King Edward I's reign in England and up to the beginning of World War I (1901-1914)

much of the literature during this time focused on the vast gap between rich and poor as well as the pitiable social conditions prevalent in British society

notable writers during this time were Joseph Conrad, E.M. Forster, Henry James, Rudyard Kipling, George Bernard Shaw, H.G. Wells, and William Butler Yeats

Elizabethan Age	refers to the span of Queen Elizabeth I's reign in England (1558-1603)
	much of the literature during this time was designed for popular entertainment and tribute to the queen and included lyric poetry, sonnets, and drama
	notable writers during this time were Shakespeare, Christopher Marlowe, Thomas Wyatt, and Sir Walter Raleigh

English Literary Renaissance	spans the Elizabethan, Jacobean, Caroline, and Commonwealth eras in English literature

épater les bourgeois (ey pah TAY lay boor ZHWAW)	a manner of writing that has the purpose to shock the sensibilities of the middle class; often used by the **avant-garde**

episteme (EPP ih steem)	a widely accepted grouping of styles, traditions, and topics that define a given literary period or movement [*see also* genre]

experimentalism	a literary concept of exploration and risk-taking; often, this involves deviating from or abolishing traditional conventions and subject matter [*see also* avant-garde, Dadaism, expressionism, Futurism, iconoclast, Modernism]

expressionism	a literary commitment to passionately expressing personal feeling, emotion, and imagination, and violently rejecting reason and reality, as expressed in naturalism and literary realism [*see also* avant-garde, Dadaism, experimentalism, Futurism, Modernism]

fin de siècle (FAN duh see EK luh)	refers to the attitudes of late 19th century writers, most notably Oscar Wilde, who rejected the notion of art serving a moral or didactic purpose and preferred, rather, to promote the aesthetic value of art and literature; from "end of the century" (French) [*see also* art for art's sake, Aestheticism and Decadence, Symbolists]
Fireside Poets	refers to a group of poets from Boston in the 19th century who wrote popular poetry that followed common conventions and was easy to memorize notable poets of this group included William Cullen Bryant, Oliver Wendell Holmes, Henry Wadsworth Longfellow, James Russell Lowell, and John Greenleaf Whittier also referred to as the **Schoolroom Poets** or **Household Poets**
fleshly school	a negative term applied by the much-maligned Robert Buchanan (using the pseudonym Thomas Maitland) to the poets Dante Rossetti, Algernon Charles Swinburne, and William Morris for being morally corrupt and overly sensual in their writings
Fugitives, the	a group of Southern poets and critics who advocated traditionalism and regionalism the members of this group were Donald Davidson, John Crowe Ransom, Allen Tate, and Robert Penn Warren

Futurism	a movement of the early 20th century that reveled in burgeoning technology and attempted to replicate the speed and power of this technology in literature
	this movement experimented with unconventional typography, meaningless sounds, and fiercely advocated the power of machines, violence, and war
	not to be confused with the term *futuristic*, which describes literature that is set in the future (often in science fiction)
	[*see also* avant-garde, Dadaism, Vorticism]

| **Georgian Period** | refers to the poetry published in five anthologies (titled *Georgian Poetry*) edited by Edward Marsh from 1912 to 1922 |
| | notable writers during this time were Robert Graves, A.E. Houseman, and D.H. Lawrence |

Harlem Renaissance	refers to the literary movement of the 1920s and 1930s based in the New York City neighborhood of Harlem
	the focus of this movement was African heritage awareness and the significance of the Black experience in America
	notable figures of this movement include Countee Cullen, Langston Hughes, and Claude McKay
	also referred to as the **New Negro** or the **Black Renaissance**
	[*see also* Négritude]

| **Hebraism/Hellenism** (HEE bray izm / HELL uh nizm) | an term devised by Matthew Arnold to describe the competing aspects of conscience (Hebraism) and spontaneity (Hellenism) combined to seek order and purpose |

humanism   a philosophy that centers on mankind's potential and importance in the universe; viewed as a departure from a spiritual view of man's place in the universe to a more worldly view

Imagism   an early 20th century movement that valued precise words that conveyed clear images

the most prominent writers of this movement were Richard Aldington, H.D. (Hilda Doolittle), F.S. Flint, T.E. Hulme, D.H. Lawrence, Amy Lowell., and Ezra Pound

[*see also* Objectivism]

Jacobean Age   refers to the span of King James I's reign in England (1603-1625)
(JAK uh bee un)

compared to the Elizabethan Period, much of the literature during this time focused on darker themes

notable writers during this time were Shakespeare, Ben Jonson, and John Donne; this was also the period in which the King James Version of the Holy Bible was published

Lake Poets   refers to William Wordsworth, Samuel Taylor Coleridge, and Robert Southey, who were Romantic poets from the Lake District in England and who were criticized as a group by the *Edinburgh Review*

Lost Generation, the   a literary movement that immediately followed World War I and refers to expatriated writers in Paris who expressed disillusionment and cynicism about traditional values and beliefs

notable authors and poets of this movement include Sherwood Anderson, John Dos Passos, F. Scott Fitzgerald, Ernest Hemingway, Ezra Pound, and Waldo Peirce

McOndo

a late 20th century Latin American literary movement that rejects the use of magical realism widely used in Latin American works and relies instead on realistic, even mundane, settings and imagery

the term is a pun on Macondo, a fictional town in Gabriel Garcia Marquez's *One Hundred Years of Solitude*, which pioneered the use of magical realism

Magic Realism

initially used by critic Franz Roh to describe artwork that presents ordinary objects in a subtle, factual but extraordinary way (known as **New Objectivity**)

more often used in connection with modern fiction writing, chiefly of South and Central America, in which elements of the supernatural or fantastical coincide with reality

also referred to as **Magical Realism**

a prominent example is Gabriel Garcia Marquez's *One Hundred Years of Solitude*

other novels that have been given this label are Angela Carter's *Nights at the Circus* and Salman Rushdie's *The Satanic Verses*

Metaphysical poetry

refers to 17th century poetry that is notable for its originality and intellectual cleverness, often achieved through the use of paradoxes, conceits, and complex themes

notable Metaphysical poets include John Donne, George Herbert, and Andrew Marvell

Middle English Period

refers to the period from 1066 to around the 15th century

notable works from this time are Chaucer's *The Canterbury Tales* and the Pearl Poet's *Sir Gawain and the Green Knight*

also referred to as the **Medieval Period**

Modernism	refers to the movement that began during World War I and lasted through World War II (1914-1945)
	this movement is a general term that encompasses many other movements, styles, and techniques; essentially, the common thread is disillusionment, a focus on experimentation, and alternate perceptions of reality
	notable British writers of this movement were Samuel Beckett, T.S. Eliot, James Joyce, and Virginia Woolf
	notable American writers of this movement were William Faulkner, Robert Frost, Ernest Hemingway, Langston Hughes, Zora Neale Hurston, and John Steinbeck
	[*see also* Harlem Renaissance, the Lost Generation]
Movement, the	a poetic movement in 1950s Britain that focused on traditionalism and rationalism as a reaction against the earlier **New Apocalypse Movement**
	notable poets of this movement were Kingsley Amis, Donald Davie, Thom Gunn, Elizabeth Jennings, Philip Larkin, and John Wain
Naturalism	refers to a 19th century literary movement that espoused a belief that life was subject to the objective and inexorable forces of nature
	notable writers of this movement include Theodore Dreiser, Jack London, and Frank Norris
Négritude (NAY grih tood)	the affirmation of independence and validity of African-American culture as a powerful force in art and literature
	[*see also* Harlem Renaissance]

Neoclassical Period

spans the **Restoration Age**, the **Augustan Age**, and the **Age of Sensibility** in English literature

much of the literature during this time focuses on balance, reason, and form, all of which was to be modeled after the Greek and Roman classics

also referred to as the **Age of Enlightenment** or **Age of Reason**

[*see also* Classicism, rationalism]

Neo-Platonism

(NEE oh PLAY toh nizm)

a third to fifth century CE philosophy that derived from the ancient Greek philosopher Plato's conception of Form and Ideal, that is, the known (finite) and the unknown (infinite)

neoplatonic philosophy countered earlier Platonic thought, which essentially espoused a dichotomy between Form and Ideal; rather, Neo-Platonism focuses on the attainment of the Ideal within the finite world of Form or human existence

also spelled **neoplatonism**

[*see also* Platonism]

Neo-Realism

refers to a mid-19th century Italian literary movement highlighting the reality, rather than a fictionalized account, of poverty

notable writers of this movement include Carlo Levi, Cesare Pavese, and Elio Vittorini

New Apocalypse Movement

a poetry movement of 1940s Britain containing elements of surrealism and anarchism

notable poets of this movement include G.S. Fraser, James Findlay Hendry, Dylan Thomas, and Henry Treece

nouveau roman

(noo VOH roh MAHN)

a term applied to mid-19th century French literature to denote a departure from conventional notions of what constitutes a novel, particularly with respect to plot and characterization; from "new novel" (French)

notable writers of this type included Michel Butor, Alain Robbe-Grillet, and Nathalie Sarraute

Objectivism

an early 20th century literary style that sought to view the poem as an object, that is, a structure, and to attain greater precision in one's poetry

notable objectivist poets were George Oppen, William Carlos Williams, and Luis Zukovsky

[*see also* Imagism]

Old English Period

refers to the period from 449 to 1066 AD, the period of Celtic prominence in England until the conquest of England by William the Conqueror

the literature of this time was dominated by oral tradition

the most notable work of this time is the epic poem *Beowulf*, which was recorded by an unknown author; two known Old English Period poets, who wrote on religious themes, were Caedmon and Cynewulf

also referred to as the **Anglo-Saxon Period**

Ossianism

(OSS ee uh nizm)

the fascination with ancient Celtic life, originating from James Macpherson's mid-18th century translation and publishing of two epic poems, *Fingal* and *Temora*, which were actually a mix of Gaelic ballads and Macpherson's own writings

[*see also* Preromanticism]

Oulipo

(ooh LEE poh)

mid-19th century literature and poetry, pioneered by Raymond Queneau, which incorporated language and mathematical games, particularly the lipogram

philosophes (FEEL oh zoffs)	refers to the leading French writers of the 18th century who advanced the notions of reason and skepticism; from "philosophers" (French) notable philosophes were Baron de Montesquieu, Jean-Jacques Rousseau, and Voltaire
Platonism (PLAY toh nizm)	the ancient Greek philosopher Plato's conception of Form and Ideal, that is, the known (finite) imperfect world representing what is unknown (infinite) and perfect elements of Platonism are reflected in literature that links physical beauty to spiritual perfection or features the concept of true (nonsexual) love, referred to as Platonic love [*see also* Neo-Platonism]
Postmodernism	refers to the movement that began after World War II and continues to present day Postmodernism extends many aspects of modernist experimentation while rejecting others, like the search for meaning in a chaotic world the blending of genres (a type of pastiche) is common sometimes referred to as **Po-Mo** or **PoMo** notable writers of this movement include Maya Angelou, Margaret Atwood, Ray Bradbury, Sandra Cisneros, Allen Ginsburg, Jack Kerouac, Salman Rushdie, and Kurt Vonnegut [*see also* Beat Generation, magic realism, pastiche, theater of the absurd]

Pre-Raphaelites

(pree RAFF ee uh lites)

a movement that occurred during the earlier part of the Victorian Period (1848-1860) and was begun by a group of young English writers and painters (the Pre-Raphaelite Brotherhood)

the philosophy of this movement was to resist artistic conventions of the time and to instead implement conventions used before the time of Italian Renaissance artist Raphael

literature of this movement favors sensuality, symbolism, and the ballad form and was influenced much by the work of Edmund Spenser

notable writers of this movement include Christina Rossetti, her brother Dante Gabriel Rossetti, and George Meredith

Preromanticism

a broad term that includes movements preceding the Romantic period and generally refers to the transition from neoclassicism to romanticism

[*see also* Ossianism, primitivism, Sturm und Drang]

Primitivism

(PRIM ih tih vizm)

an 18th and 19th century literary focus on nostalgia and all things rural and uncivilized

a prominent theme is the superiority of the so-called "noble savage" over civilized man, a concept developed by Jean-Jacques Rousseau, an influential primitivist

[*see also* Preromanticism]

Realism

refers to a style of writing, popularized in the 19th century, that focuses on depicting life accurately and without any hint of idealism or fantasy

notable writers of this style were Willa Cather, Stephen Crane, and George Eliot

also referred to as **literary realism** or **verism**

Restoration Age	refers to the restoration of the monarchy and the span of King Charles II's reign in England (1660-1700)
	much of the literature during this time focused on restoring reason over passion
	notable writers during this time were John Locke, John Dryden, and John Milton
Romantic Period	refers to the time from 1785 to 1830 in British literary history
	much of the literature during this time focused on nature, the exploration of feelings and passion, as well as mystery, melodrama, and the supernatural
	also referred to as **romanticism**
	notable writers during this time were Mary Shelley, John Keats, Jane Austen, Lord Byron, Samuel Taylor Coleridge, and William Wordsworth
	[*see also* American Romanticism]
Shavian	a term that refers to works created by the poet/author George Bernard Shaw
socialist realism	the literary doctrine of the Marxist regime during the early to late twentieth century aimed to reinforce the ideals of socialist dogma, including rigid limits on style and an overriding theme of a classless society
	Examples representing this doctrine:
	Mother (Maxim Gorky)
	Cement (Fyodor Gladkov)
Sturm und Drang (SHTOORM oont DRANG)	a late 18th century literary movement in Germany that countered neoclassical ideas and served as a basis for romanticism with a focus on individualism; from "storm and stress" (German)
	[*see also* Preromanticism]

Surrealism (sur REEL izm)	literary movement of the 1920s that followed Dadaism surrealist poets and authors attempted to express the subconscious using techniques such as stream of consciousness, dream sequences, free association, and whimsical imagery
Symbolists (SIM boh lists)	a group of late 19th century French poets who attempted to meld the musicality of verse with the suggestive elements of mood and imagery, particularly with the use of free verse, prose poetry, and synesthesia notable poets of this group include Stephane Mallarme, Arthur Rimbaud, and Paul Verlaine
theater of the absurd	refers to several dramas of the 1950s that focused on the absurdity and meaninglessness of human existence (an underlying tenet of **existentialism**) also referred to as **absurdist drama** notable playwrights of this nomenclature include Edward Albee, Samuel Beckett, Eugène Ionesco, and Harold Pinter
theater of cruelty	refers to the belief of French dramatist Antonin Artaud that the theater must profoundly affect the audience; this effect is primarily achieved through gestures and staging rather than through dialogue
Transcendentalism (tran sin DENT ih lizm)	a movement in mid 19th century America that coincided with the American Romantic period Transcendentalists revered nature and intuition and saw these as the basis for higher meaning and universal truth notable Transcendental writers include Ralph Waldo Emerson and Henry David Thoreau

Wertherism (VURR durr izm)	a period of self-absorbed depression that was fashionable in the late 18th century due to the sentimental novel *The Sorrows of Young Werther*, written by J.W. Von Goethe
Victorian Period	refers to the time during Queen Victoria's reign in England (1837-1901) much of the literature during this time focused on social conditions and reform this period included the following movements: The Pre-Raphaelites (1848-1860) and the movement of Aestheticism and Decadence (1880-1900) notable writers during this time were Charlotte Bronte, Charles Dickens, Thomas Hardy, Alfred, Lord Tennyson, and Oscar Wilde
Vorticism (VOHR tih sizm)	an early 20th century off-shoot of Imagism that called for the abolition of sentimentality in literature and celebrated dynamism, violence, and the power of industrialization [*see also* avant-garde, Futurism, Modernism]
zeitgeist (TSAHYT gahyst)	the prevailing cultural and moral climate of a generation or an era; from "spirit of the time" (Greek)

abjection	a term coined by philosopher Julia Kristeva to denote the act of rejecting things that are reviled because they are not part of the natural order of things; a key component in horror writing in that the reader is forced to confront that which should be avoided
alienation effect	a principle set forth by Bertolt Brecht that advocates the detachment of an audience from the play they are watching and, often, the actors from the characters they are portraying
	methods include allowed audience interruptions, reminders that the play is fictional, and frequent staging changes
	also referred to as the **A-effect** or **V-effekt**
alterity (al TARE ih tee)	a description of the distinctions between one's self and others; a critical concept in developing a frame of reference that includes other cultures and their ideas
anxiety of influence	a concept described by literary critic Harold Bloom to describe the relationship between poets and their forerunners, particularly with respect to the competing aspects of admiration yet desire to break free from the traditions and styles used by the earlier generation
	this notion, rooted in Freudian philosophy, is manifested by the later poet imitating but then reforming the work of the earlier poet in order to claim a dominance as father (the earlier poet) yields his position to the son (later poet)
	Bloom's examples of this concept include the succession of John Milton to William Wordsworth and then William Wordsworth to Percy Shelley, with each later poet initially accepting then rejecting the poetic traditions of the earlier poet
	[*see also* misprision]

atmosphere of the mind	a term coined by Henry James to describe what a writer is trying to convey to the reader, particularly the subjective feelings and sensations of writing
autotelic (awe toh TELL ik)	a concept from New Criticism literary theory that espouses the notion that a literary work's purpose is simply to exist and not to have any other purpose (symbolic, didactic, aesthetic, or otherwise); from "self completing" (Greek)
binary opposition	the categorization of literary elements into pairs of contrasting elements, which rely upon each other for definition (e.g., black/white, man/woman, cold/hot, etc.) a key aspect of structuralism, which advocates an orderly sorting of ideas, symbols, and texts
biographical criticism	a method of literary analysis that takes into account the details of an author's life
Cambridge School	an influential group of University of Cambridge literary critics in the early 20th century who advocated an analytical, close reading of the text itself rather than a historical or biographical analysis notable members of this group included William Empson, F.R. Leavis, Q.D. Leavis, and I.A. Richards [*see also* dissociation of sensibility, New Criticism, practical criticism]

Chicago School   a group of mid-20th century University of Chicago literary critics who used principles that the ancient Greek philosopher Aristotle presented in his work *Poetics*

these principles include the analysis of text as a whole and the placement of the text with respect to its genre as well as a focus on the connection between form and content

notable members of this group included R.S. Crane, W.R. Keast, Elder Olson, and Bernard Weinberg

also referred to as the **Chicago critics** or **Neo-Aristotelians**

comparative literature   the analysis of the same literary work written in different languages to ascertain distinctions among cultures

criteria   a set of standards used to analyze or evaluate a work or body of works

one standard on its own is a **criterion**

criticism   the interpretation and analysis of literature

[*see also* explication]

crux
(CRUKS)   a critically important passage in a text upon which interpretation and analysis rests

cultural criticism   a critical approach that looks at all aspects of the literature and art of a society, from high culture to popular culture

this approach incorporates various schools of thought, including, but not limited to, deconstructionism, gender studies, and New Historicism

cultural materialism a type of literary analysis in which a work's economic and social impact are heavily analyzed

also refers to the analysis of how a work is interpreted and staged with respect to current social and cultural institutions

notable cultural materialists include Catherine Belsey, Jonathan Dollimore, and Alan Sinfield

[*see also* New Historicism]

deconstruction

(dee kun STRUK shun)

an approach to literary criticism first espoused by Jacques Derrida that challenges the notion that a text can have a singular meaning; thus, deconstruction is the close, critical disassembling of a text's purported meaning to expose contradictions and multiple, varied, and non-confirmable meanings

deep structure the essential meaning of a text; that is, its content meaning

contrasted by the text's form (e.g., syntax, diction, etc.), which is referred to as **surface structure**

defamiliarization

(dee fuh mill yuh RAY shun)

the effect of a work to break a long-standing perception or conventionality

[*see also* alienation effect, formalism, Russian Formalism]

dialogic a term coined by critic Mikhail Bakhtin to describe a work that contains multiple voices and is not dominated by one single voice (known as **monologic**)

[*see also* intertextuality, polyphonic]

différance

(diff er AHNTS)

Jacques Derrida's term used in deconstructionism to describe the indefinable nature of any term without the use of other terms; also, that no element of language has a meaning in and of itself but rather just a distinction based on other words

dissemination

(dih sim ih NAY shun)

a literary concept advanced by literary critic Jacques Derrida to denote the infinite meanings of words and concepts in a text

[*see also* différance, indeterminacy]

dissociation of sensibility

(diss soh see AY shun)

a concept in critical literary analysis ascribed by T.S. Eliot disapprovingly to poets who separated thought from feeling in their poetry

dogma

(DOG mah)

an inflexible, rigid adherence to a certain doctrine or theory

egotistical sublime

a pejorative term John Keats used to describe William Wordsworth's poetry, which Keats felt was self-centered

[*see also* negative capability]

Electra complex

(eh LEK truh KAHM pleks)

a psychoanalytic label that describes a female's repressed, unconscious desire for her father and antipathy toward her mother

attributed to the Greek legend of Electra, who took part in the murder of her mother, who was responsible for the murder of Electra's father King Agamemnon

also referred to in modern slang as **daddy issues**

[*see also* Freudian criticism, Oedipus complex, psychoanalytic criticism]

empiricism

(em PEER ih sizm)

a critical literary approach that depends on observation and experience rather than on an established literary theory

[*see also* rationalism]

énoncé/énonciation

(EY nahns EY/EY nahns see EY shun)

terms to denote the differentiation of the speaker from that which is spoken

énoncé is that which is spoken, and the énonciation is the speaking

these terms are critical pieces of **post-structuralist theory** in which the speaker is often differentiated from the subject

Example:

"I knew I should not have gone into that room."
The **énonciation** is the narrator's voice, and the stated knowledge of the earlier self is the **énoncé**.

exegesis

(eks uh JEE sus)

an explanation or interpretation, especially of the Bible

explication

(eks plih KAY shun)

an analysis of a literary work's language and form in order to infer its meaning

[*see also* criticism]

fabula

a practice in Russian Formalism to view the essential elements of a story as distinct from each other

[*see also* sjuzet]

fabulation

a critical term to describe modern fiction that is unabashedly creative in its use of traditional literary conventions

feminist criticism

a broad, generally late 20th century, literary philosophy that seeks to highlight the female perspective and the patriarchal social structure that marginalizes women and their contributions

foregrounding	within the scope of literary criticism, the practice of making some aspect of a work more prominent over others (e.g., a concrete poem makes the form of a poem more prominent than the underlying meaning of the poem; also, the diction of local color writing may be more prominent than other elements in a work)
formalism	a broad term applied to literary construction or theory that emphasizes form over subject matter, including language, structure, and style
	notably, the work itself is the focus of criticism, to the exclusion of historical or cultural influences
	also referred to as **Formalist criticism**
	[*see also* Russian Formalism]
formulaic	a literary work that follows an established pattern of literary conventions, stock characters, or of the genre itself
four levels of meaning	a critical literary approach advanced by 14th century Italian poet Dante Alighieri to classify four underlying meanings or interpretations of a text: allegorical, anagogical, historical, and moral
Freudian criticism (FROID ee un)	a 20th century critical literary approach that relies on the study of the unconscious themes conveyed in a text by the author as a manifestation of the author's hidden, subconscious desires
	[*see also* psychoanalytic criticism]

Geneva School	a critical literary movement, starting at the University of Geneva in the mid-20th century, that aimed to identify with an author's mode of consciousness throughout his or her works
	an underlying focus is to analyze the works first to get a sense of the author's consciousness
	[*see also* biographical criticism]
gender criticism	a critical approach that focuses on distinctions between male and female as well as the sociological/cultural influences that define the roles of each and, thus, how they are presented in a text
	[*see also* feminist criticism, Queer Theory]
grammatology	a study of language that includes, as an underlying tenet, a critique of phonocentrism, which is the belief that speech is more important than the written word
	[*see also* deconstruction]
gynocriticism	literary criticism that focuses on women as writers
(GAHY noh KRIT ih sizm)	contrast with **feminist criticism**, which focuses more on how male authors portray women in literature
hermeneutics	the study of theories of interpretation
(her muh NOO tiks]	the process of analyzing a text by anticipating the work as a whole and then analyzing the parts of text as they relate to the whole is known as a **hermeneutic circle**
higher criticism	a close analysis of a text, particularly the Holy Bible as a historical document, with an intense focus on authorship and sources as well as cultural and historical contexts
	[*see also* textual criticism]

horizon of expectations	a term coined by literary critic Hans Robert Jauss to describe a set of assumptions and expectations that a reader has when evaluating a text at a given time [*see also* reader-response criticism]
implied reader	a term used in reader-response criticism to denote the supposed ideal reader of a text; that is, the reader for whom the text is meant to address this is contrasted by the **actual reader**, who has his or her own experiences and assumptions and, thus, may not read the text as it was intended
Impressionistic criticism	literary criticism that relies on general feelings and impressions rather than on a particular school of thought
indeterminacy (in dih TERM ih nih see)	a critical theory that says parts of a text can be interpreted in a variety of ways and, thus, depend on the reader's interpretation for the literary effect
intentional fallacy	a term used by New Critics to describe a mistaken assumption that one can evaluate a work by assuming what the author's intentions were when creating it; rather, according to the New Critic approach, the text itself should be analyzed with no such filter
interpolation (in TURR poh LAY shun)	an unauthorized passage inserted into a work, usually by a later editor
interpretation	a reader's perception of the author's meaning or the literary effects used in a text

intertextuality

(IN turr teks tew AL ih tee)

a term coined by philosopher Julia Kristeva to describe the notion that all literature is interconnected and interdependent, and, thus, the interpretation of literature relies on the comparative analysis of a text with other similar texts

Jungian criticism

(YOONG ee un *or* JOONG ee un)

a 20th century critical literary approach that relies on the study of the what philosopher Carl Jung termed the **collective unconscious**, which consists of the shared experiences and symbols of all cultures, past and present (called literary archetypes)

according to Jung, literary texts are the expression of the core themes of these unconscious, shared experiences and symbols

[*see also* archetype, psychoanalytic criticism]

Lacanian criticism

(luh KAY nee un)

a 20th century critical literary approach based on Jacques Lacan's view that human perception and the unconscious are shaped by the symbolic order of language rather than in the so-called "imaginary" order of pre-linguistic thought

[*see also* psychoanalytic criticism]

langue/parole

(LAHNG / puh ROLE)

terms used in structuralist criticism to denote the grammatical and linguistic conventions of a language (langue) and the actual language being spoken (parole)

structuralists view the langue as having a higher priority over parole due to its overarching impact on parole

linguistics

(lin GWISS tiks)

the analysis of language, including aspects of etymology, morphology, phonetics, semantics, and syntax

literati

(lit uh RAH tee)

a term used to describe the educated elite, but often in a disparaging way to indicate some type of pretention on the part of the scholar

logocentrism

(loh guh SIN trizm)

a critical literary approach that focuses on the structure and meanings of words of a text rather than on the historical or biographical contexts of the text

[*see also* phonocentrism, structuralism]

Marxist criticism

(MARK sist)

generally speaking, a critical approach that focuses on subtexts and hidden meanings, particularly related to political themes and social class struggles

developed from the political, economic, and philosophical bases of Marxism

[*see also* sociological criticism]

metacriticism

(MAY tih KRIT ih sizm)

a critical literary approach that analyzes literary criticism in and of itself

metalanguage

(MAY tuh LANG gwij)

language and terms used in the analysis of language itself

misprision

(miss PRIZH un)

a term used by literary critic Harold Bloom to describe a poet's intentional creative misinterpretation of an earlier poem in order to break free from his or her predecessor's influence in order to create a distinct identity

[*see also* anxiety of influence]

mythological criticism

a critical literary approach that analyzes archetypes and underlying patterns of literature and how these patterns span various disparate cultures and create a universality of meaning

also referred to as **archetypal criticism**

[*see also* archetype, leitmotif, motif, myth, Jungian criticism]

negative capability a term coined by Romantic poet John Keats to describe the belief that poets have certain inherent limitations in understanding the world and, as a result, must delve themselves into their subject matter automatically and extemporaneously

New Criticism an early to mid-20th century critical literary approach established by John Crowe Ransom that criticized the use of social or historical perspective in the analysis of literature and focuses, rather, on a close analysis of the text itself

[*see also* autotelic, Cambridge School, formalism, intentional fallacy, practical criticism]

New Historicism
(NOO hih STORE ih sizm)

a late 20th century critical literary approach advanced by Stephen Greenblatt and is rooted in the focus on historical context, particularly the dominant social and cultural values of the time, in the analysis of literature

New Humanism an early 20th century critical literary approach that valued conservative literary and moral values and rejected the tenets of **naturalism**

notable New Humanist critics included Irving Babbitt and Paul Elmer More

objective correlative a term popularized by early-20th century poet T.S. Eliot to describe a symbol or situation that explicitly represents a mood or emotion rather than simply a suggestion

Oedipus complex

(ED ih puss KAHM pleks)

a psychoanalytic label that describes a male's repressed, unconscious desire for his mother and antipathy toward his father

attributed to the Greek legend of Oedipus, who unknowingly murdered his father and married his mother (*Oedipus the King*, Sophocles)

[*see also* Electra complex, Freudian criticism, psychoanalytic criticism]

paleography

(pay lee OGG ruh fee)

the deciphering and interpretation of ancient manuscripts and inscriptions

phenomenological

(fih nom uh noh LAHJ ih kul)

a critical literary approach that relies on the reader's perceptions rather than any external influences

[*see also* reader-response criticism]

phonocentrism

(foh noh SIN trizm)

a belief that speech is a more important linguistic activity than writing

[*see also* logocentrism]

postcolonial criticism

a critical approach that analyzes the literature that has been produced by authors living in a previously colonized region

the focus of such literature is usually to expose the colonizing power's cruelty toward the indigenous people in relation to the colonized region or its ignorance of the culture of the indigenous people

post-structuralism

a late 20th century critical literary approach that relies on an ever-changing variety of perspectives and meanings rather than on the rigid principles of structuralism

[*see also* énoncé/énonciation, deconstruction, Lacanian criticism, structuralism]

practical criticism	a term advanced by I.A. Richards to describe a critical literary theory that aims to closely analyze literature in a raw form with no coloration from historical or biographical influences
	[*see also* Cambridge School, New Criticism]
prescriptive criticism	establishing standards of what a literary work should contain within a certain genre or under specific circumstances
	contrast with **descriptive criticism**, which is an analysis of a work based on previously established standards or norms
psychoanalytic criticism	literary criticism that is aimed at closely analyzing texts by first analyzing the unconscious impulses and desires in shaping human behavior and expression
	[*see also* archetype, Freudian criticism, Jungian criticism, and Lacanian criticism]
Queer Theory	a subset of gender criticism that closely scrutinizes and challenges traditional views of gay and lesbian identities in literature
	heavily influenced by Michael Focault's *La Volonté de savoir* from the late 20th century
	[*see also* gender criticism]
rationalism	a belief that reason alone best guides humanity; also, that an orderly structure of reality can be formed through reason, which is the chief source of knowledge
	[*see also* empiricism, Neoclassical Period]

reader-response criticism	a critical literary approach that relies on reader interpretation more than the literature itself to ascertain meaning [*see also* hermeneutics, horizon of expectations, psychoanalytic criticism, structuralism]
reception theory	a critical literary approach related to reader-response criticism but is more concerned with a text's meaning in a contemporary sense and the changes in interpretation over time
reductionism	the breakdown of a text's complex meaning to a simpler one, often to the point of drawing out archetypes
reflectionism	a literary concept that views a text as a mirror of reality
Russian Formalism	an early 20th century critical literary approach that advocated the scientific analysis of literary devices used in a text [*see also* formalism, structuralism]
semiotic literary criticism (see mee OTT ik)	a critical literary approach that relies upon the interpretation of how symbols (particularly language) convey a text's meaning; from "signs" (Greek)
signifier/signified	terms coined by Ferdinand de Soussure to differentiate between a symbol or word (signifier) from the thing being represented (signified—also known as the **referent**) even if there is no inherent link between the two **Example:** The letters *c*, *a*, and *t* arranged in that particular order are a signifier that creates an image or conceptualization (the signified). This meaning has no linguistic basis but simply rests on the fact that it is different than other arrangements of letters which form other meanings.

sjuzet

(syoo ZHET)

the plot of a narrative as presented to the reader, as opposed to the actual chronological order or duration

also spelled **suzet** or **syuzhet**

[*see also* fabula, Russian Formalism]

sociological criticism

a critical literary approach that examines relationships and social constructs within literature and determines the role of the literature in a larger social context

[*see also* feminist criticism, Marxist criticism]

structuralism

a mid-20th century critical literary approach that viewed literature as interconnected without regard for external interpretation and relied on formally established, distinct categorizations of ideas, symbols, and texts

[*see also* binary opposition]

textual criticism

the study of existing manuscripts to ascertain the most accurate representation of a text; also refers to any close textual analysis of literature

[*see also* higher criticism]

transcendental signified

a term used to denote an ultimate fixed point as a basis of meaning in language analysis; this concept is derided in post-structuralist criticism because it is argued that there can be no objective fixed point of reference because all interpretations are limited by their own critiques and limitations of language and meaning

[*see also* deconstruction]

typology

(tahy POL uh jee)

the practice of interpreting the Hebrew scriptures as they relate to the New Testament of the Holy Bible, particularly how the prophecies and events reflect the life and Messianic manifestation of Jesus; this practice was particularly popular during the Medieval Period

allusion (uh LOOZH un)	reference to a historical, mythical, or literary figure, event, or narrative **Examples:** "Dwayne fought with **Herculean** strength." (Reference to the Greek hero Hercules). "'Maybe **the hairs of my head were numbered**,' she went on with sudden serious sweetness, 'but nobody could ever count my love for you.'" ("The Gift of the Magi," O. Henry; Reference to Luke 12:7). "Getting him away from his friends is his **Achilles heel**. Without them, he isn't so tough." (Reference to the Trojan warrior Achilles's vulnerable spot.) "The more I think about it, old Billy was right / **Let's kill all the lawyers**, kill 'em tonight" ("Get Over It," The Eagles, referring to the line "The first thing we do, let's kill all the lawyers" from *Henry VI, Part II*, IV.ii, Shakespeare [note: *Billy* is a common nickname for *William*])
adynaton (uh DIN uh tahn)	a type of hyperbole that states the impossibility of expressing something in order to emphasize it **Examples:** "There are no words that can express how much I love you." "It is easier for a camel to pass through the eye of a needle, than for a rich man to enter into the kingdom of God." (Matthew 19:24)
amphiboly (am FIB uh lee)	an ambiguous statement (i.e., one having multiple or confusing meanings) due to the grammatical structure of a statement (includes misplaced or dangling modifiers); also, prophecies with double meanings **Examples:** "I stood by my friend crying." 　　[It is not clear who cried.] Be bloody, bold, and resolute; laugh to scorn The power of man, for none of woman born Shall harm Macbeth. (the three witches' prophecies to Macbeth in Shakespeare's *Macbeth*, IV.i)

anachronism

(uh NAK kroh nizm)

a character or some other plot element placed in an inappropriate time; from "against time" (Greek)

Examples:

> Reference to the University of Wittenberg in Shakespeare's *Hamlet* and a reference to clocks in Shakespeare's *Julius Caesar*, both of which did not exist at the time of the setting of these respective plays, are anachronisms.

> Some movies have intentional anachronisms; for example, *The Flintstones* (1994) (modern appliances), *Moulin Rouge* (2001) (20th century songs); and *Romeo + Juliet* (1996) (set in 20th century).

analogy

(uh NAL uh jee)

a comparison of two dissimilar things to show that they are alike in some respects (often expressed as similes, metaphors, or allegories), or

the comparison of two pairs of words that have the same relationship

an **extended analogy** is a comparison that spans several lines or throughout the entire work

Example:

> "hot is to cold as fire is to ice"

antapodosis

(ann toh poh DOH sis)

an extended analogy; a comparison in multiple respects; from "giving back" (Greek)

Example:

> "If Jennifer were a state, she'd be Hawaii—she's laid back, cool, and has a language of her own."

anthimeria

(an thuh MARE ee uh)

using one part of speech to act as another; such as using a noun or adjective as a verb; from "instead of" (Greek)

Examples:

> "I'm tired of this committee—I'm all **meetinged** out!"
> "Can you **blue** this paint up a bit?"

anthropopatheia

(ANN throh poh pah THEE uh)

assigning human emotions or attributes to God

Examples:

"But the Lord God called to the man, **'Where are you?'** He answered, 'I heard you in the garden, and I was afraid because I was naked; so I hid.' And He said, **'Who told you that you were naked? Have you eaten from the tree that I commanded you not to eat from?'**" (Genesis 3:9-11)

"**God Walks** These Hills with Me" (Eddy Arnold)

[*see also* anthropomorphism, personification]

anthropomorphism

(ann thruh poh MORE fizm)

a type of personification in which deities, animals, or other non-humans are described in human form and as having human qualities; from "form of man" (Greek)

Examples of works featuring anthropomorphism:

Aesop's fables

"The Nun's Priest Tale" (Chaucer)

The Jungle Book (Rudyard Kipling)

Animal Farm (George Orwell)

Additionally, many African, Egyptian, Greek, Native American, and Roman myths feature anthropomorphic gods and animals.

[*see also* anthropopatheia, personification]

antiphrasis

(ann TIFF ruh sis)

figurative language that features a word used in its opposite sense and is meant as irony or sarcasm; from "opposite word choice" (Greek)

Examples:

"She sure is in a **happy** mood!" – referring to a person who is actually in a bad mood

The noble Brutus
Hath told you Caesar was ambitious:
If it were so, it was a grievous fault,
And grievously hath Caesar answer'd it.
Here, under leave of Brutus and the rest--
For Brutus is an **honourable man**;
So are they all, all **honourable men**--
Come I to speak in Caesar's funeral.
He was my friend, faithful and just to me:
But Brutus says he was ambitious;
And Brutus is an **honourable man**.
(*Julius Caesar*, III.ii, Shakespeare)

antithesis

(an TIH thuh sis)

a statement or concept that is the direct opposite of another statement or concept

Example:

> "She is the light of my future, not the darkness of my past."

antonomasia

(an tahn oh MAY zhuh)

an epithet or more commonly understood name that replaces a proper name; also the use of a particular proper name to refer to someone with similar qualities

Examples:

> the **Bard** for Shakespeare; **His Holiness** for a pope; **Casanova** for a ladies' man
>
> "The **black prince**, sir; alias, the **prince of darkness**; alias, the devil." (*All's Well That Ends Well*, IV.v, Shakespeare)
>
> "I am no great **Nebuchadnezzar**, sir; I have not much skill in grass." (*All's Well That Ends Well*, IV.v, Shakespeare)
>
> "And it is that promise that 45 years ago today brought Americans from every corner of this land to stand together on a Mall in Washington, before Lincoln's Memorial, and hear **a young preacher from Georgia** speak of his dream." ("Democratic Candidate Acceptance Speech," Barack Obama, 2008)

apostrophe

(uh POSS troh fee)

addressing something that is abstract or someone or something that is not physically present; from "a turning away" (Greek)

Examples:

> "Frailty, thy name is woman!" (*Hamlet*, I.ii, Shakespeare)
>
> "Hail, Holy Light, offspring of heaven firstborn!" (*Paradise Lost*, Book III, John Milton)

asterismos

(ass turr EEZ mohs)

an introductory word intended to focus attention on what follows

Examples:

> "**Behold**, thou hast driven me out this day from the face of the earth" (Genesis 4:14)
>
> "And the angel said unto them, Fear not: for, **behold**, I bring you good tidings of great joy, which shall be to all people." (Luke 2:10)
>
> "**Hey**, wait up!"

auxesis

(okk SEE sis)

a form of hyperbole in which the speaker lists items in ascending order of importance; also, exaggerating something for the purpose of amplifying its seriousness or importance

Examples:

"My duty is my **family**, my **country**, and to **God**."

"And if a voice can change a **room** it can change a **city**. And if it can change a city it can change a **state**. If it can change a state it can change a **country**, and if it can change a country it can change the **world**." ("Presidential Campaign Speech," Barack Obama, 2007)

catachresis

(kat uh KREE sis)

a mixed metaphor or the incorrect or improper use of a word, such as using a word out of context; also referred to as **abusio** (ab YOO see oh)

Examples:

"Can't you hear that? Are you blind?"

"To take arms against a sea of troubles." (*Hamlet*, III.ii, Shakespeare)

"Baseball is 90% mental, the other half is physical." (Yogi Berra)

catch-22

a term used to indicate a situation that is mutually exclusive to a situation that requires it; a paradox that cannot be resolved

from the Joseph Heller novel *Catch-22*, in which a self-contradictory rule poses a no-win situation

Examples:

"You can't get a job without experience, but you can't get experience unless you have a job."

"We will dunk this woman under the water. If she should not drown, then she is a witch, and we shall burn her alive. If she should drown, then she was innocent."

cliché

(klee SHAY)

an overused or trite expression

Examples:

"in the blink of an eye"

"last but not least"

[*see also* snowclone]

conceit	an elaborate and clever metaphor
(kun SEET)	**Example:**

> If they be two, they are two so
> As stiff twin compasses are two;
> Thy soul, the fixed foot, makes no show
> To move, but doth, if th' other do.
> And though it in the centre sit,
> Yet when the other far doth roam,
> It leans, and hearkens after it,
> And grows erect, as that comes home.
> Such wilt thou be to me, who must
> Like th' other foot, obliquely run;
> Thy firmness makes my circle just,
> And makes me end, where I begun.
> ("A Valediction Forbidding Mourning," John Donne)

[*see also* Petrarchan conceit]

---

controlling metaphor

a metaphor that gives shape to an entire work

sometimes referred to as a **central metaphor**

Example:

> Well, son, I'll tell you:
> Life for me ain't been no crystal stair.
> It's had tacks in it,
> And splinters,
> And boards torn up,
> And places with no carpet on the floor --
> Bare.
> ("Mother to Son," Langston Hughes)

[*see also* extended metaphor, metaphor]

---

dead metaphor

a phrase, once recognized as a metaphor, that has become so familiar that it is no longer recognized as a metaphor

Examples:

> "three branches of government"
> "eye of a needle"

double entendre

(DUB ull un TAHN druh)

a phrase or word that can be interpreted in one of two ways, but often the alternate meaning is one with a sexual connotation; from "double meaning" (French)

Examples:

The word *utopia* universally means "perfect place," but in actuality, its Greek origins mean "nowhere place."

"A nudist camp is simply a place where men and women meet to air their differences."

epic simile

an extended simile elaborated in much detail

often called a **Homeric simile** (ho MARE ik SIM uh lee) due to its frequent use in Homer's epic poems

Example:

So godlike Hector prompts his troops to dare;
Nor prompts alone, but leads himself the war.
On the black body of the foe he pours;
As from the cloud's deep bosom, swell'd with showers,
A sudden storm the purple ocean sweeps,
Drives the wild waves, and tosses all the deeps.

(*The Iliad*, Book XI, Homer)

epithet

(EPP uh thet)

a descriptive word or phrase connected to a particular person, place, or thing; can also refer to a vulgarity or obscene term

Examples:

"Peter **the Great**"

"Richard **the Lion-Hearted**"

"America **the Beautiful**"

"I've been looking for **Mr. Right** all my life."

[*see also* antonomasia]

euphemism

(YOO fuh mizm)

a softened version of a harsh word or phrase

related terms include **minced oath**, which is an alteration of a profane word for mainstream use (e.g., *heck, dang, darnit*) and **dyspemism** (also referred to as **cacophemism**), a deliberate harshening of a more agreeable term so as to shock or offend (e.g., "that's crap" for "that's not acceptable," "snail-mail" for traditional, standard mail delivery)

Example:

"passed away" for "died"

"enhanced interrogation" for "torture"

---

extended metaphor

a metaphor elaborately developed throughout the work

also referred to as a **sustained metaphor**

Example:

Shall I compare thee to a summer's day?
Thou art more lovely and more temperate.
Rough winds do shake the darling buds of May,
And summer's lease hath all too short a date.
Sometime too hot the eye of heaven shines,
And often is his gold complexion dimmed;
And every fair from fair sometime declines,
By chance, or nature's changing course untrimmed.
But thy eternal summer shall not fade
Nor lose possession of that fair thou ow'st;
Nor shall death brag thou wand'rest in his shade,
When in eternal lines to time thou grow'st,
So long as men can breathe or eyes can see,
So long lives this, and this gives life to thee.
("Sonnet 18," Shakespeare)

[*see also* conceit, controlling metaphor, metaphor]

---

figure of speech

a non-literal expression used for literary or rhetorical effect; also referred to as **figurative language**

[*see also* scheme, trope]

hyperbole

(hahy PURR buh lee)

an exaggeration or overstatement; from "over throwing" (Greek)

Examples:

"Ben has the appetite of a starving lion."

"You've got a million chances to get this right!"

hypocorism

(hahy POK uh rizm)

using diminutives or pet-names; from "to play the child" (Greek)

also referred to as **terms of endearment**

Examples:

"sweetie," "honey," "Mikey," "Tiny Tim"

idiom

(ID ee um)

an expression that cannot be translated literally from one language to another; also, a way of speaking and writing specific to a particular group

Examples:

"to follow suit"

"kick the bucket"

"back in the day"

implied metaphor

a comparison that is not as clearly stated as a regular metaphor, requiring a closer analysis

Examples:

"What leaf-fringed legend haunts about thy shape" (John Keats)

irony

a contradiction between appearance or expectation and reality

cosmic irony—an implication in plot or events that humans are mere playthings for the gods or for Fate

Example:

Thomas Hardy's *Tess of the d'Urbervilles* extensively illustrates through Tess's story elements of cosmic irony, how Fate controls almost every aspect of her life, especially noted in the last paragraph:

"A few minutes after the hour had struck something moved slowly up the staff, and extended itself upon the breeze. It was a black flag. 'Justice' was done, and the President of the Immortals, in Aeschylean phrase, had ended his sport with Tess." (*Tess of the d'Urbervilles*, Thomas Hardy)

dramatic irony—failure of a character to see or understand what is revealed to the audience (also referred to as **tragic irony**)

Example:

A notable example of dramatic irony occurs in Shakespeare's *Hamlet* (III.iii) when Hamlet spares the life of Claudius because he thinks Claudius is praying. Hamlet believes that killing Claudius during prayers would actually reward Claudius by sending him straight to heaven. Little did Hamlet know (but the audience soon finds out), Claudius reveals that he was not able to repent and was not truly praying.

HAMLET	Now might I do it pat, now he is praying;
	And now I'll do't. And so he goes to heaven;
	And so am I revenged. That would be scann'd:
	A villain kills my father; and for that,
	I, his sole son, do this same villain send
	To heaven.

	To take him in the purging of his soul,
	When he is fit and season'd for his passage?
	No!
	Up, sword
CLAUDIUS	My words fly up, my thoughts remain below:
	Words without thoughts never to heaven go.

irony *(cont.)*

romantic irony—the self-awareness of an author in his or her work, usually to address the style or conventions of the work (sometimes in a self-deprecating manner)

Example:

> Most epic poets plunge "*in medias res*"
> (Horace makes this the heroic turnpike road),
> And then your hero tells, whene'er you please,
> What went before -- by way of episode,
> While seated after dinner at his ease,
> Beside his mistress in some soft abode,
> Palace, or garden, paradise, or cavern,
> Which serves the happy couple for a tavern.
> That is the usual method, but not mine --
> My way is to begin with the beginning;
> (*Don Juan*, Canto I, George Gordon, Lord Byron)

situational irony—the difference between what the audience or reader expects to happen and what actually happens

Examples:

> In Shirley Jackson's "The Lottery," the reader may expect the winner of the lottery to gain financially, but the so-called winner is actually stoned to death.

> In the movie *The Sixth Sense* (1999), Dr. Malcolm Crowe, a child psychologist who tries to help a young boy who apparently sees ghosts, is revealed at the end of the movie as a ghost himself, something he, and the audience, don't know until the point of revelation.

Socratic irony—pretending to be ignorant of an issue in order to ask probing questions that are intended to expose the weaknesses of an argument

verbal irony—saying the opposite of what is meant or what is expected

Examples:

> "For Brutus is an honourable man; So are they all, all honourable men" (*Julius Caesar*, III.ii, Shakespeare) [This line from Marc Antony is delivered as he turns the crowd against Brutus and the other conspirators.]

litotes

(lahy TOH teez *or* LAHY tuh teez)

a figure of speech that expresses an understatement by stating the negative of its opposite; from "simple" (Greek)

Examples:

"Well, he's **not a bad** singer."

"I am **not unaware** of your predicament."

"If you can tell the fair one's mind, it will be **no small proof** of your art, for I dare say it is more than she herself can do." (*The Guardian*, Alexander Pope)

meiosis

(mahy OH sis)

a figure of speech in which a reference to something belittles it or reduces its importance, either with a diminished word or euphemism

also referred to as **tapinosis** or **understatement**

Examples:

"That knife wound is just a scrape."

"New York–a little town on a little island in a river."

"It isn't very serious. I have this tiny little tumor on the brain." (*Catcher in the Rye*, J.D. Salinger)

"Last week I saw a woman flayed, and you will hardly believe how much it altered her person for the worse." ("A Tale of a Tub," Jonathan Swift)

[*see also* litotes]

metallage

(meh TAL uh jee)

using an expression within another expression; from "taking over in exchange"

Examples:

"We have to find out which job candidate has the 'I want to help the company' attitude."

"I'm tired of your 'I can't' and 'I won't.'"

metaphor (MET uh fore)	comparing one thing to an unlike thing without using *like*, *as*, or *than* composed of two parts: the **tenor**, which is the subject of the metaphor, and the **vehicle**, the object that is being compared

Examples:

"**She** is the **sunshine** of my life."

"And the **tongue** is a **fire**, a **world of iniquity**:" (James 3:6)

"**Life** for me ain't been **no crystal stair**." ("Mother to Son," Langston Hughes)

[*see also* controlling metaphor, extended metaphor, implied metaphor, mixed metaphor, simile]

metonymy (muh TAHN uh mee)	a figure of speech that replaces the name of something with an attribute or common association; from "a change of name" (Greek)

Examples:

"The **White House** issued a statement condemning Iran's nuclear ambitions." [*White House* represents the President of the United States]

"The **pen** is mightier than the **sword**." [*pen* represents the act of writing, and *sword* represents the act of fighting]

"I am he that liveth, and was dead; and, behold, I am alive for evermore, Amen; and have the **keys** of hell and of death." (Revelation 1:18) [*keys* represents authority]

[*see also* synecdoche]

mixed metaphor	a comparison that is illogical, or two or more metaphors used incorrectly

Examples:

"Wake up and smell the music."

"He's up a tree without a paddle."

[*see also* Farberism, metaphor, Yogiism]

oxymoron

(oks see MORE ahn)

two seemingly contradictory words placed side by side that offer a truth or some other poetic expression; an oxymoron is a form of **paradox**; from "pointedly foolish" (Greek)

Examples:

> "Parting is such **sweet sorrow**." (*Romeo and Juliet*, II.ii, Shakespeare)
>
> "No light; but rather **darkness visible**" (*Paradise Lost*, Book I, John Milton)
>
> "I do here make **humbly bold** to present them with a short account of themselves and their art." ("A Tale of a Tub," Jonathan Swift)

[*see also* synoeciosis]

palindrome

(PAL in drome)

a word, sentence, or verse that reads the same either backward or forward

Examples:

> "Madam, I'm Adam."
>
> "A man, a plan, a canal—Panama!"
>
> "Evil, all its sin is still alive" (*The Poisonwood Bible*, Barbara Kingsolver)

paradox

(PAIR uh doks)

contradictory statement that may actually be true

a paradox is similar to an oxymoron in that both figures of speech use contradictions to state a truth; however, a paradox does not place opposing words side by side, as an oxymoron does

Examples:

> "But many that are first shall be last; and the last shall be first." (Matthew 19:30)
>
> "For slaves, life was death, and death was life."

[*see also* oxymoron, synoeciosis]

paraprosdokian

(pare uh proze DOKE ee un)

a figure of speech in which the last part of a sentence or phrase is unexpected and often gives a humorous or double meaning; from "faulty expectation" (Greek)

Examples:

"If I am reading this graph correctly – I would be very surprised." (*The Colbert Report*, Stephen Colbert)

"You can always count on Americans to do the right thing — after they've tried everything else." (Winston Churchill)

Petrarchan conceit

(puh TRARK kun kun SEET)

an exaggerated comparison or **paradox** used in **Petrarchan sonnets**, often to describe a suffering lover's relationship to his lover

Examples:

I would
Love you ten years before the Flood;
And you should, if you please, refuse
Till the conversion of the Jews.

("To His Coy Mistress," Andrew Marvell)

Some lovers speak when they their Muses entertain,
Of hopes begot by fear, of wot not what desires:
Of force of heav'nly beams, infusing hellish pain:
Of living deaths, dear wounds, fair storms, and freezing fires.

("Astrophel and Stella," Sir Philip Sidney)

pleonasm

(PLEE uh nazm)

using more words than may be necessary to express an idea; redundancy; from "excessive" (Greek)

Examples:

"I saw the wound; I saw it with mine eyes." (*Romeo and Juliet*, III.ii, Shakespeare)

"My husband is a married man."

"Tis so. And the tears of it are wet." (*Antony and Cleopatra*, II.vii, Shakespeare)

[*see also* tautology]

pun	play on words; using a word that sounds like another word but having a different meaning, often creating a humorous effect
	also referred to as **paronomasia** or a **jeu de mots** (ZHEH duh MOH)

Examples:

"Marriage is a wife sentence."

"They went and told the sexton and the sexton tolled the bell." (Thomas Hood)

scheme	a figure of speech that involves word forms and order, syntax, and sounds (e.g., alliteration, anastrophe, assonance, and ellipsis); from "form" (Greek)

Example:

"Ask not what your country can do for you; ask what you can do for your country."("Inaugural Address," John F. Kennedy, 1961)

[*see also* trope]

simile (SIM ih lee)	comparing one thing to an unlike thing using *like*, *as*, or *than*

Examples:

"The barge she sat in, like a burnished throne, burned on the water." (*Antony and Cleopatra*, II.ii, Shakespeare)

"And the muscles of his brawny arms / Are strong as iron bands." ("The Village Blacksmith," Henry Wadsworth Longfellow)

"In the morning the dust hung like fog, and the sun was as red as ripe new blood." (*The Grapes of Wrath*, John Steinbeck)

"Float like a butterfly, sting like a bee." (Muhammad Ali)

[*see also* metaphor]

syllepsis

(suh LEP sis)

a device in which a single predicate applies to two or more parts of a sentence but lacks grammatical correctness or takes on a different meaning with one; from "a taking" (Greek)

syllepsis is a type of zeugma

Examples:

> "She has deceiv'd her father, and may thee." (*Othello*, I.iii, Shakespeare)

> "We must all hang together or assuredly we will all hang separately." (Benjamin Franklin)

> "You held your breath and the door for me." ("Head over Feet," Alanis Morrisette)

synecdoche

(suh NEK duh kee)

a figure of speech by which a part is used to represent the whole

Examples:

> "The Confederates have **eyes** in Lincoln's government." [The word *eyes* stands for spies]

> "Not marble, nor the gilded monuments / Of princes, shall outlive this powerful **rhyme**..." ("Sonnet 55," Shakespeare) [The word *rhyme* refers to the poem as a whole]

[*see also* metonymy]

synesthesia

(sin us THEEZ yuh)

a concurrent sensation of one sense but in terms of another sense (e.g., an expression of color (visual) through sound (auditory)); from "perceiving together" (Greek)

Examples:

> "That was a **loud** Hawaiian shirt you wore yesterday!"

> "The **scent** of the bread **hummed** through the kitchen."

> "**blue** uncertain stumbling **buzz**" (Emily Dickinson)

synoeciosis

(sin ih SEE ih sis)

an extended paradox; a collection of contrary statements meant to supplement, not conflict, each other

Examples:

> "For to me to live is Christ, and to die is gain." (Philippians 1:21)

> "To sue to live, I find I seek to die; / And, seeking death, find life: let it come on." (*Measure for Measure*, III.i, Shakespeare)

[*see also* oxymoron, paradox]

transferred epithet

a figure of speech in which a modifier (an epithet) is applied to one noun when it should be applied to another (a displaced modifier); a type of **hypallage**

Examples:

"It was another **sleepless night**."

"This was a **tiring day**."

"He raised the house with **loud and coward cries**." (*King Lear*, II.iv, Shakespeare)

"Alas, what **ignorant sin** have I committed?" (*Othello*, IV.ii, Shakespeare)

"The plowman homeward plods his **weary way**," ("Elegy Written in a Country Churchyard," Thomas Gray)

trope

a figure of speech in which a word or phrase is used in a non-literal way (e.g., metaphor, double entendre, metonymy); from "turn" (Greek)

Example:

"I am the bread of life." (John 6:35)

[*see also* scheme]

zeugma

(ZOOG mah)

a figure of speech in which a single predicate applies to two or more other parts of a sentence; from "to yoke" (Greek)

Examples:

"We must also imagine the perpetrator so vacillating an idiot as to **have abandoned** his **gold** and his **motive** together." ("The Murders in the Rue Morgue," Poe, Edgar Allan)

"How Tarquin **wronged** me, I Collatine." (*The Rape of Lucrece*, Shakespeare)

"Nor Mars his **sword** nor war's quick **fire shall burn** / The living record of your memory." ("Sonnet 55," Shakespeare)

"**Kill** the **boys** and the **luggage**" (*Henry V*, IV.vii, Shakespeare)

[*see also* hypozeugma, mesozeugma, prozeugma, syllepsis]

acronym

(AK ruh nim)

a memorable term or phrase created by using the first letters (initials) of multiple words

Examples:

> **laser** (light amplification by stimulated emission of radiation)
> **OPEC** (Organization of Petroleum Exporting Countries)
> **radar** (radio detection and ranging)

[*see also* acrostic, backronym, RAS Syndrome]

---

antisthecon

(an TISS thuh kahn)

substituting a word, letter, syllable, or word part for another word, letter, syllable, or word part

Examples:

> "I **resemble** [resent] that remark."
> "A pun is its own **reword** [reward]."
> "And I **wuv** [love] you too!"

---

antonym

(AN tuh nim)

words that have opposite meanings

Examples:

> "happy" / "sad"
> "lost" / "found"
> "hot" / "cold"

[*see also* synonym]

---

aphaeresis

(aff AIR rhee sis)

the omission of a first letter, syllable, or word part, usually for the sake of rhythm; also spelled **apheresis**

Example:

> "The King hath cause to **plain**." (*King Lear*, III.i, Shakespeare)
> [In this example, *plain* is *complain*.]

---

apocope

(uh POK uh pee)

the omission of a last letter, syllable, or word part, usually for the sake of rhythm; from "to cut off" (Greek)

Example:

> "Season your admiration for awhile / With an **attent** ear." (*Hamlet*, I.ii, Shakespeare)
> [In this example, *attent* is *attentive*.]

[*see also* syncope]

backronym

a recently coined term to describe a phrase that is created to invent an acronym from an existing word; a backward acronym of sorts, often useful as a mnemonic device

Examples:

> Roy G. Biv (for the sequence of colors in the visible spectrum of light: red, orange, yellow, green, blue, indigo, violet)
>
> USA PATRIOT Act (Uniting and Strengthening America by Providing Appropriate Tools Required to Intercept and Obstruct Terrorism)

capitonym

(kah PIT oh nim)

a word that changes its pronunciation and meaning when capitalized

Examples:

> "August" / "august" (AWE gust / awe GUST)
> "concord" / "Concord" (KAHN cord / KAHN kurd)
> "polish" / "Polish" (PAHL ish / POH lish)

diaeresis

(dahy AIR uh sis)

the separation of a syllable into two parts; often indicated by a diacritical mark; from "taking apart" (Greek)

Examples:

> "noël," "naïve"

[*see also* synaeresis]

diphthong

(DIP thawng)

a vowel sound that slides from a distinct beginning to a distinct ending, usually from the merging of two vowels, or, simply, a digraph (two vowels)

Examples:

> b**oy**; b**oi**l; l**ou**d; s**ea**t

[*see also* monophthong]

elision

(uh LIZH un)

the slurring or omission of an unstressed syllable, usually by fusing a final unstressed vowel with a following word beginning with a vowel or mute *h*, usually for the sake of rhythm

Example:

> "Th' expense of spirit." ("Sonnet 129," Shakespeare)

epenthesis

(eh PEN thuh sis)

the insertion of a letter or sound in the middle of a word, often as a matter of dialect or to accommodate meter; from "insertion" (Greek)

Examples:

pronouncing "umbrella" as "um buh rella"

pronouncing "sherbet" as "shur burt"

pronouncing "athlete" as "ath uh lete"

---

grapheme

(GRAFF eem)

the most basic unit of any written language; usually a letter, digit, punctuation mark, or symbol

[*see also* phoneme]

---

heteronym

(HET ehr oh nim)

a word that has the same spelling as another word but with a different pronunciation and meaning (a type of homograph)

Examples:

"row" (to move a boat, pronounced ROH) / "row" (a fight, pronounced RAHW)

"desert" (to abandon, pronounced deh ZERT) / "desert" (a dry region, pronounced DEZ ert)

---

homograph

(HOH moh graff)

two or more words identical in spelling but having different meanings

[*see also* heteronym, homonym]

---

homonym

(HAHM uh nim)

a word that has the same pronunciation and spelling as another but with a different meaning (a type of homograph)

Examples:

"bark" – the sound a dog makes or the outer layer of a tree

"deal" – to distribute cards in a card game or a bargain

homophone
 	
(HAHM uh fone)
	words that have the same pronunciation but different spellings and meanings; from "same sound" (Greek)
	Examples:
	    "they're" / "their"
	    "plain" / "plane"
	    "knight" / "night"

logogram	a letter, character, or symbol that represents a word or concept without providing a phonetic breakdown of the individual phonemes
	
	also referred to as an **ideogram**
	Examples:
	    & (*and*)
	    $ (*U.S. dollar*)
	    € (*Euro*)

monophthong (MON uff thawng)	a singular vowel sound **Examples:** bad; rot; sand
morpheme (MORE feem)	the smallest linguistic unit within a language that has meaning
morphology (more FAWL uh jee)	the study of word formations and patterns

oronym
 	
(ORE uh nim)
	a homophonic phrase
	Examples:
	    "**I scream** for **ice cream**."
	    "**Some others** I've seen." / "**Some mothers** I've seen."

paragoge

(pair uh GOH jee)

the addition of an extra syllable or letter to the end of a word

Examples:

"It's time to go beddy-**bye**."

"Go before, nurse: commend me to thy lady; / And bid her **hasten** all the house to bed," (*Romeo and Juliet*, III.iii, Shakespeare)

---

phoneme

(FOH neem)

a basic unit of sound in a language; from "speech sound" (Greek)

[*see also* grapheme]

---

phonetics

(foh NET iks)

the study of physical sounds used in human speech

---

phonology

(fuh NALL uh jee)

the study of sound systems and patterns used in specific languages

diachronic phonology is the analysis of pronunciation changes over time in a particular language

synchronic pronology is the analysis of pronunciation at a single point in the development of a specific language

---

polysemous

(pol ee SEE muss)

a word having multiple meanings

[*see also* homograph, homonym]

---

prothesis

(PROH thes sis)

adding an extra letter or syllable to the beginning of a word, usually for the sake of rhythm; from "to put before" (Greek)

also referred to as **prosthesis** (pross THEE sis)

Examples:

"Old fond eyes, / **Beweep** this cause again, I'll pluck ye out," (*King Lear*, I.iv, Shakespeare)

"By going to Achilles. / That were to **enlard** his fat-already pride." (*Troilus and Cressida*, II.iii, Shakespeare)

RAS Syndrome

(RASS SIN drome)

the redundant use of a word that is already part of the acronym in an acronym phrase

Examples:

ATM machine (**a**utomated **t**eller **m**achine *machine*)

PIN number (**p**ersonal **i**dentification **n**umber *number*)

UPC code (**u**niversal **p**roduct **c**ode *code*)

---

retronym

(REH troh nim)

a term created to describe an earlier thing or concept that requires more specificity after which a term to describe later versions has become widely used

coined by journalist Frank Mankiewicz

Examples:

camera to *film camera* (as opposed to *digital camera*)

guitar to *acoustic guitar* (as opposed to *electric guitar*)

oven to *conventional oven* (as opposed to *microwave oven*)

---

seme

(seem)

a basic unit of description

---

sesquipedalian

(sess kwih puh DAY lee un)

a word containing many syllables or one who uses long words

---

synaeresis

(sin AIR eh sis)

combining two syllables or two normally separate vowels into one; from "putting together" (Greek)

Examples:

"Nawlins" for "New Orleans"

"Nyawk" for "New York"

"seest" for "see est"

[*see also* diaeresis]

---

syncope
 	
(SINK kuh pee)
	the omission of a letter, sound, or syllable within a word (rather than from the beginning or end of the word, which is elision); from "cutting short" (Greek)
	
	a type of **hyphaeresis**, the omission of a letter, sound, or syllable from any part of a word
	
	Examples:
	    "heav'n" for "heaven"
	    "o'er" for "over"
	
	[*see also* apocope]

synonym
 	
(SIN uh nim)
	words that have similar meanings
	
	Examples:
	    "happy" / "thrilled"
	    "stop" / "halt"
	    "hot" / "balmy"
	
	[*see also* antonym]

tautonym (TAW toh nim)	a word that consists of two identical syllables **Examples:** "bye-bye," "paw-paw," "tutu," "yo-yo," "da-da"

tmesis
 	
(tih MEE sis)
	placing a word or phrase in between a compound word or two syllables; from "to cut"
	
	Examples:
	    "Intended or committed was this fault? / If on the first, **how heinous <u>e'er</u> it** be, / To win thy after-love I pardon thee." (*Richard II*, V.iii, Shakespeare)
	    "un-**bloody**-believable"
	    "any-**old**-how"

a fortiori (ah fore tee OR ee)	speaking from a position of strength; the argument that one should accept a claim because a stronger claim has been proven **Examples:** "If I can serve as Governor, I can certainly serve as mayor." "This should be easy for you; my two-year-old son can do that!"
a priori (ah prahy OR ee *or* ah pree OR ee)	basic, fundamental assumptions or assertions that can be accepted without evidence or experience contrast with **a posteriori** (ah poh steer OR ahy), which are assertions dependent upon evidence or experience
a propos (ah pruh POH)	pertinent; related to the topic being discussed
abstract generalization	a non-precise representation of a concept
accident fallacy	a logical fallacy in which a generalization is applied to a case in which an exception should be applied also referred to as **destroying the exception** **Example:** "Students are not allowed to hit others while at school, so all football players will be suspended indefinitely." [*see also* converse accident fallacy, slippery slope]
accismus (ak SIS muss)	pretending to not want something while actually wanting it; being coy; from "affectation" (Greek) **Examples:** "Oh, you shouldn't have." "I couldn't possibly accept such an expensive gift!" "Then he / offered it to him again; then he put it by again: / but, to my thinking, he was very loath to lay his / fingers off it." (*Julius Caesar*, I.ii, Shakespeare)

ad hominem argument (add HAHM uh nim)	attacking an opponent's character rather than supporting or refuting an actual position **Examples:** "My opponent is wrong because he's uneducated and foolish."
ad populem argument (add POP yoo lim)	insisting that because other people support a proposition, argument, or product, so should the audience as well also referred to as the **bandwagon appeal** **Example:** "Ask your doctor about Botox—most women have already made the wise choice to do so."
adianoeta (ah dee ah noh EE tah)	an expression that has a hidden meaning in addition to the apparent meaning **Examples:** "The executives of the soap company want to clean out Wall Street." "Margie will bring forth the same leadership as our last president." [the suggestion here is that the last president was a weak leader]
adynaton (ah DIN ah ton)	an exaggerated expression of impossibility **Examples:** "I will sooner have a beard grow in the palm of my hand than he shall get one of his cheek" (*Henry IV, Part 2*, I.ii, Shakespeare) "I wouldn't go out with you even if you were the last woman on earth!"
amphidiorthosis (am fee dahy or THOH sis)	dodging an attack by qualifying what one says **Example:** "I'm not saying you're fat. I'm just saying your dress doesn't flatter you."

ampliatio

(AM plee AH tee oh)

using a label to categorize someone or something after the label is no longer valid, appropriate, or understood within mainstream contemporary society

Examples:

> "He may have voted with the Republicans on this bill, but Senator Jones is still a **bleeding-heart liberal**."

> "The ladies might have liked you in high school, but you're no **James Dean** now."

[*see also* antonomasia]

anamnesis

(AN am NEE sis)

bringing up a past issue to support an argument

Example:

> "The thousand injuries of Fortunato I had borne as I best could, but when he ventured upon insult I vowed revenge." ("The Cask of Amontillado," Edgar Allan Poe)

[*see also* apomnemonysis]

anoiconometon

(ah noi koh noh MEE tahn)

poorly arranged words with a confused meaning

Example:

> "Hence, although the imagination is not dazzled in the conquest of Florida, with descriptions of boundless wealth and regal magnificence—although the chiefs are not decked in 'barbaric pearls and gold'—their sturdy resistance, and the varied vicissitudes created by the obstacles which nature presented to the conqueror's march, afford numberless details of great interest." (*A Conquest of Florida*, Edgar Allan Poe)

antanagoge

(AN tah NAH go jee)

illustrating a difficult situation in a positive way; from "against a leading up" (Greek)

often referred to in modern media as **spin**

Examples:

> "But we, we happy few, we band of brothers; / For he today that sheds his blood with me / Shall be my brother" (*Henry V*, IV.iii, Shakespeare)

> "We may lose this vote, but at least the community will know that we stood up for them!"

anthypallage

(an thih PALL ah jee)

changing the grammatical case within a sentence for emphasis

Example:

> ""**I** told myself, '**You** need to get your act together!'"

[*see also* **enallage**]

---

antilogy

(ann TIH loh jee)

a contradiction within a speech or literary work by an author or speaker; from "against knowledge" (Greek)

Example:

> "I actually did vote for the $87 billion before I voted against it." (John Kerry, U.S. presidential candidate, 2004)

---

antirrhesis

(ann turr RHEE sis)

categorically rejecting an opinion or a person

Examples:

> "The judge has no right to do this! She's a fraud, and this is a kangaroo court!"

> "Politicians are nothing but cheats and liars."

> "True! —nervous – very, very dreadfully nervous I had been and am; but why will you say that I am mad? The disease has sharpened my senses – not destroyed – not dulled them. Above all was the sense of the hearing acute. I heard all things in the heaven and the earth. I heard many things in hell. How, then, am I mad?" ("The Tell-Tale Heart," Edgar Allan Poe)

[*see also* apodioxis]

---

antisagoge

(ann tiss uh GOH jee)

offering a negative consequence before offering one's point or presenting alternating consequences for positive and negative situations; from "balancing arguments" (Greek)

Examples:

> "We may lose this fight, but we have to continue fighting."

> "Vote for this bill and you will help support the economy. Don't support the bill, and you will help plunge this country into a depression."

antistasis

(ann TISS tay sis)

the repetition of a word or phrase in which the latter meaning changes from the first; from "resistance" (Greek)

also referred to as **antanaclasis** (ANN tan uh KLASS sis)

Examples:

"If you aren't **fired** with enthusiasm, you will be **fired** with enthusiasm." (Vince Lombardi)

"The recession was **fueled** by the soaring price of **fuel**."

apagoresis

(ah pah GORE ee sis)

a declaration intended to prevent someone from doing something; a threat; from "to dissuade" (Greek)

Examples:

"If you go in that room, you're not going to come out."

"If you start this fight, I'm going to finish it."

apocarteresis

(ah poh kar tih REE sis)

giving up hope in one thing and putting that hope in something else

Examples:

"We may have lost the battle, but we can still win the war!"

"Well, Julie won't go out with me, but there are other girls I can ask."

apodioxis

(app oh dahy OKS iss)

rejecting an opponent or his argument as out of touch, absurd, or evil

Examples:

"How can you, of all people, question my motives?"

"That we know more about global warming today than we did five years ago is ridiculous."

[*see also* antirrhesis]

apodixis

(ah poh DIKS iss)

an assertion based on the belief something is common or general knowledge; from "proof" (Greek)

Examples:

"Why would I steal your iPod? Everyone knows that I already have the newest model."

"Well, he certainly should not be dating her. Everyone knows that it's not right for a high school senior to be dating someone in junior high."

apomnemonysis

(ah pom nim oh NAHY sis)

citing an authority from memory to support one's argument

Examples:

> "Wasn't it Patrick Henry who said, 'Give me liberty or give me death.'?"

> "Would Gandhi or Dr. Martin Luther King approve of these tactics?"

[*see also* anamnesis]

apophasis

(ah POFF ah sis)

asserting something within a denial of saying it; from "denial" (Greek)

Examples:

> "I'm not saying that you're too talkative, but you certainly have a lot to say."

> "Wert thou not my father, I would have called thee unwise." (*Antigone*, Sophocles)

[*see also* paralipsis]

aporia

(uh PORE ee uh)

the expression of doubt by a speaker in the form of a self-directed question

also, a paradox or insolvable contradiction within a literary work; from "difficult passage" (Greek)

Examples of first definition:

> "'Well,' replied my friend, 'that is all very fair, to be sure. Let me think! – **what should I have?** Oh! I will tell you. My reward shall be this. You shall give me all the information in your power about these murders in the Rue Morgue.'" ("The Murders in the Rue Morgue," Edgar Allan Poe)

> Then live, Macduff. **What need I fear of thee?**
> But yet I'll make assurance double sure
> And take a bond of fate. Thou shalt not live!
> (*Macbeth*, IV.i, Shakespeare)

Example of second definition:

> "There is no God and we are his prophets." (*The Road*, Cormac McCarthy)

[*see also* dubitatio]

appeal to authority a rhetorical fallacy in which the truth of an assertion is based on the credibility of a supposed expert and his or her support of the claim rather than on facts or evidence

Examples:

"Leading scientists agree that this problem must be resolved now."

"The president supports this policy, so this must be the right course of action."

argument a set of premises and conclusions based on logic; the proof of a claim through logical reasoning, evidence, and examples

Aristotelian Model of Argumentation the formation of an argument to support a claim or to refute an existing claim

utilizes four elements of persuasion: **ethos**, **logos**, **pathos**, and **kairos**

the logical aspect of this model primarily involves the use of a **syllogism** or **enthymeme**

[*see also* Rogerian Model of Argumentation, Toulmin Model of Argumentation]

autoclesis

(ott oh KLEE sis)

raising interest in a subject by disingenuously stating that the subject should not be addressed or discussed; from "self invitation" (Greek)

Example:

A notable example is Marc Antony's mentioning of Caesar's will in Act III, scene 2 of Shakespeare's *Julius Caesar*. Antony states that he should not share the will with the mob because he fears that it would incite them to anger, which, of course, arouses their curiosity and incites them to anger.

ANTONY	But here's a parchment with the seal of Caesar;
	I found it in his closet, 'tis his will:
	Let but the commons hear this testament--
	Which, pardon me, I do not mean to read--
	And they would go and kiss dead Caesar's wounds
	And dip their napkins in his sacred blood,
	Yea, beg a hair of him for memory,
	And, dying, mention it within their wills,
	Bequeathing it as a rich legacy
	Unto their issue.
CITIZEN	We'll hear the will: read it, Mark Antony.
ALL	The will, the will! we will hear Caesar's will.
ANTONY	Have patience, gentle friends, I must not read it;
	It is not meet you know how Caesar loved you.
	You are not wood, you are not stones, but men;
	And, being men, bearing the will of Caesar,
	It will inflame you, it will make you mad:
	'Tis good you know not that you are his heirs;
	For, if you should, O, what would come of it!
CITIZEN	Read the will; we'll hear it, Antony;
	You shall read us the will, Caesar's will.

[*see also* paralipsis]

autophasia

(ah toe FAY zhuh)

a rhetorical device that refers back to itself, particularly as a contradiction; from "the speaking of oneself"

Examples:

"If you're illiterate, read the following brochure for help."

"My last email to you was concerning the dangers of technology."

barbarism

(BAR bar izm)

using a non-standard word or pronunciation, often denoting ignorance or indifference

Examples:

"nukular" for "nuclear"

"prolly" for "probably"

"mercy buckups" for "merci beaucoup" (mare SEE boo KOO)

[*see also* cacozelia]

bombhiologia

(BOM fee oh LOH jee uh)

self-aggrandizing language; from "bombastic language" (Greek)

Examples:

"If it weren't for me, I don't think we could have resolved this bill."

"I am so cool."

cacemphaton

(kah KEM fuh tahn)

a foul or vulgar expression

Examples:

"Well, that just sucks."

"This meeting is a bunch of crap."

cacosyntheton

(cak oh SIN thih thahn)

poorly formed speech; from "badly formed" (Greek)

Examples:

"You are telling me that way because why you're not sure how to tell me."

"Don't think that I'm not no good negotiator for the company."

cacozelia (kak oh ZEEL ee yah)	a misappropriation of foreign words or phrases in an effort to sound educated **Examples:** "Well, as they say, tempus forgets it, time flies!" [should be *tempus fugit*] [*see also* barbarism]
charientismus (KAR ee in TISS muss)	easing a harsh statement with gentle mockery **Examples:** "Don't bite my head off, please." "If I'm such a danger, lock me up immediately." [*see also* sarcasm]
circular reasoning	a logical fallacy in which a conclusion is reached by relying on an assumption made in the same argument also referred to as **begging the question**; the formal term is **petitio principii** (peh TIH tee oh prin SIH pee) **Examples:** "The defendant is guilty because he is the one on trial." "Obviously, BMWs are for snobs because the people who drive BMWs are snobs." "The greatest thing about Product X is that it is the best product on the market."
circumlocution	indirect, wordy, ambiguous, or evasive language also referred to as **periphrasis** (puh RIF ruh sis) **Examples:** "The manner in which you are speaking, at least indirectly, is, at best, representative of an attempt to belabor the inevitability of addressing the central issue at hand" [*rather than "Get to the point."*] "Most sacrilegious murder hath broke ope / The Lord's anointed temple, and stole thence / The life o' the building!" (*Macbeth*, II.iii, Shakespeare) [[*rather than "Someone murdered King Duncan!"*] "Son of God" [*rather than "God's son"*]

cohortatio

(koh hohr TOT ee oh)

bringing up a opponent's past mistakes to discredit or ridicule him

Example:

> Wallace: When Kerry said, "I voted for the $87 billion before I voted against it"?
>
> Rove: Disbelief….We immediately turned it into a revised version of the ad that featured an ending with those words on it. And it's the gift that kept on giving.
>
> [Presidential adviser Karl Rove upon being asked about his strategy to use a statement by presidential candidate John Kerry against him, 2004]

commoratio

(kahm more AH tee oh)

repeating one's strongest argument for emphasis

Example:

> "You can't go out with him. He's a jerk. He won't treat you right, and you deserve better than that."

[*see also* epimone]

contrarium

(kun TRAIR ee um)

proving one thing with another in the form of an antithesis

Examples:

> "You can win the voters' approval by losing the election."
> "Can we not prevail in this battle that we are afraid to fight?"

converse accident fallacy

a logical fallacy in which a principle that is true for one case is wrongly applied to all cases, ignoring the exception of the original case that makes the principle true

also referred to as a **sweeping generalization**

Example:

> "If seniors are allowed to park their cars at school, then sophomores and juniors should also."

[*see also* accident fallacy, hasty generalization]

deduction	a specific conclusion based on accepted premises, often in the form of a syllogism

Example:

> All politicians are liars. (Premise)
> Mayor Smith is a politician. (Premise)
> Therefore, Mayor Smith is a liar. (Conclusion)

[*see also* induction]

---

dialectic (dahy uh LEK tik)	the art of formal reasoning and argumentation (debate)

---

dialogismus (dahy ul uh JIZ mus)	to speak as another person, either to establish a counterpoint or simply to clarify that person's viewpoints; to put words in another person's mouth; from "dialogue" (Greek)

Examples:

> "'There isn't a problem with roads right now,' the governor has said. However, I, just as you, hit pothole after pothole, and I think we need to have this problem fixed!"

> "If I were her, I would say I had nothing to do with it!"

---

dialysis (dahy AL uh sis)	an argument in which one presents alternatives in succession to a conclusion

Example:

> "You can support this candidate either because you trust her position on the issues or because you feel that she has a vision for the future. In either case, you will have made a historic decision."

---

diaphora (dahy AFF fore uh)	repeating a common name for the purpose of defining the individual being named and describing the characteristics commonly associated with the name

Examples:

> "The **teacher** was being a **teacher** when she stayed after school to help her struggling students."

> "**Boys** will be **boys**."

diaskeue (dahy az KYOO ee)	using detailed, explicit **peristasis** (description of a situation) to arouse sympathy; from "to arm; to prepare" (Greek) **Examples:** "I have no food, no shelter, no family, and no opportunity—could you spare a couple of dollars?" [*see also* emotional loading, pathos]
diasyrmus (DAHY ah seer muss)	using an absurd comparison to reject an argument **Example:** "Electing him for councilman would be like putting makeup on a pig."
diatyposis (dahy uh tahy POH sis)	a rhetorical figure in which advice is given **Examples:** "To thine own self be true" (*Hamlet*, I.iii, Shakespeare) Beware of them, Diana; their promises, enticements, oaths, tokens, and all these engines of lust, are not the things they go under: many a maid hath been seduced by them; and the misery is, example, that so terrible shows in the wreck of maidenhood, cannot for all that dissuade succession, but that they are limed with the twigs that threaten them. I hope I need not to advise you further; but I hope your own grace will keep you where you are, though there were no further danger known but the modesty which is so lost. (*All's Well That Ends Well*, III.v, Shakespeare)
digression	a moving away from one topic to another unrelated topic also referred to as **birdwalking** [*see also* excursus]

dirimens copulatio

(DIH rih mens koh poo LAH tee oh)

a rhetorical figure in which one statement is emphasized by a contrasting, qualifying statement

Examples:

"Not only should you arrive to social functions on time, you should also be prepared to arrive fashionably late."

Oh my man, I love him so!
He'll never know.
All my life is just despair
But I don't care.
("Billie's Blues," Billie Holliday)

disinformation

widespread release of false information in order to mislead or influence the public or an entity

[*see also* propaganda]

dispositio

(dis poh SIT ee oh)

the arrangement of rhetorical elements in a speech or writing; consists of six stages:

- **Introduction** (exordium)—a declaration of the speaker's assertions and the purpose of the oratory
- **Statement of Facts** (narratio)—a description of the facts surrounding the issue
- **Division** (partitio)—an outline of the points to follow
- **Proof** (confirmatio)—a presentation of logical arguments (logos) as proof
- **Refutation** (refutatio)—an answer to the opponent's counterarguments
- **Conclusion** (peroratio)—a summation and call to action, often employing emotional appeals (pathos)

[*see also* rhetoric]

dubitatio

(doo bee TAH tee oh)

a disingenuous claim of not having the ability to speak well or not knowing how to proceed in an argument

a special form of aporia

also referred to as **deliberatio** (duh lih buh RAH tee oh)

Examples:

"Ladies and gentlemen of the jury, what can I say next to defend my client? How can I possibly counter such overwhelming emotional testimony from the victim? Do you think I should show you actual evidence since no one else seems to want to?"

"I am no orator, as Brutus is; / But, as you know me all, a plain blunt man," (*Julius Caesar*, III.ii, Shakespeare)

effictio

(eff FIK tee oh)

a rhetorical figure that describes a person's body in parts

Example:

"But two of Judge Alito's supporters who participated in the murder boards, speaking about the confidential sessions on condition of anonymity for fear of White House reprisals, said they emerged convinced that his demeanor was a political asset because it gave him an Everyman appeal: **'He will have a couple hairs out of place,' one participant said. 'I am not sure his glasses fit his facial features. He might not wear the right color tie. He won't be tanned. He will look like he is from New Jersey, because he is. That is a very useful look, because it is a natural look.** He's able to go toe-to-toe with senators, and at the same time he could be your son's Little League coach.'" (*New York Times*, January 2, 2006)

[*see also* blazon]

elenchus

(ih LENG kuss)

a logical refutation

[*see also* Socratic dialogue]

emotional loading

relying on emotional appeals rather than appeals of logic and reason; a form of **pandering** (catering to the lower tastes and desires of others or exploiting their weaknesses)

while the use of pathos is often encouraged, using emotionally loaded words steers away from reasoned analysis, creating feelings of extreme emotion

Example:

> "Vote for me, and all your wildest dreams will come true." (*Napoleon Dynamite*, 2004)

enallage

(in NALL uh jee)

to replace one grammatical construction for another; from "exchange" (Greek)

only effective if done purposefully, such as to mock or deride; unintended use signifies ignorance or mis-education

Examples (purposeful):

> "My opponent sees himself as a **man's man**, but **she** would prefer arranging doilies than protecting your gun rights!"

> "The elite media might want to label me as **backwoods since I don't know how to do all that fanciful book-learning that I ain't so good at.**"

enantiosis

(uh nan tahy OH sis)

a rhetorical figure in which contrary or opposite meanings have a paradoxical or ironic effect; from "opposite" (Greek)

Examples:

> "The church contains in full the kindness and cruelty, the fierce intelligence and the shocking ignorance, the struggles and successes, the love and, yes, the bitterness and bias that make up the black experience in America." ("A More Perfect Union," Barack Obama, 2008)

> "I couldn't watch, but I couldn't look away either."

enargia (in ARE jee uh)	describing something in such a way that it seems to be happening in the moment; from "vividly visible" (Greek) also referred to as **hypotyposis** (hahy poh tahy POH sis) **Example:** "We hear the axe. We see the flame of burning cabins and hear the cry of the savage." ("The Meaning of Four Centuries," 1892, Francis Bellamy) [*see also* imagery]
ennoia (in NOI ah)	speaking with hidden meaning (often, in the form of ridicule); from "intention" (Greek) **Example:** "I'm looking forward to meeting Joe Biden. I've been looking forward to meeting him since the second grade." (Governor Sarah Palin, 44-year-old vice-presidential candidate speaking about her 65-year-old opponent, Senator Joe Biden, in 2008) [*see also* sarcasm]
enthymeme (IN thuh meem)	a shortened syllogism; deductive reasoning with implied, understood assumptions; from "in the thymus" (Greek) contains the following elements: conclusion, cause, reason **Examples:** "He must be rich because he drives a BMW." "Susan failed three of her classes, so she must not have gone to class." [*see also* syllogism]

epimone

(eh PIM oh nee)

an argument by virtue of a repetition of an appeal using the same words or in much of the same way; from "to tarry" (Greek)

Examples:

"I cannot understand why he supports this bill, but he does. I don't know why he denounces our current successful policy, but he does. Although I cannot imagine how he could hurt the country even further, I assure you he will."

The noble Brutus
Hath told you Caesar was ambitious:
If it were so, it was a grievous fault,
And grievously hath Caesar answer'd it.
Here, under leave of Brutus and the rest--
For Brutus is an **honourable man**;
So are they all, all **honourable men**--
Come I to speak in Caesar's funeral.
He was my friend, faithful and just to me:
But Brutus says he was ambitious;
And Brutus is an **honourable man**.
(*Julius Caesar*, III.ii, Shakespeare)

[*see also* commoratio]

epiphonema

(ee pee foh NEE mah)

a pithy summarization of what has just been said

Example:

The following excerpt follows Chaucer's "The Reeve's Tale" and summarizes the events (and the moral) of the story:

"Thus is the haughty miller soundly beat, And thus he's lost his pay for grinding wheat, And paid for the two suppers, let me tell, of Alain and of John, who've tricked him well, His wife is taken, also his daughter sweet; Thus it befalls a miller who's a cheat."

epiplexis

(epp ih PLEKS iss)

a rhetorical question with the intent to express frustration or to admonish; from "to strike upon" (Greek)

Example:

"Don't you think that, if you had studied the proposal, you would understand my objections?"

epitasis
 	
(eh PIT uh sis)
	an additional statement that emphasizes or makes more urgent what has been said before
	
	Examples:
	
	    "Vote this fall for a new style of leadership. Vote for change."
	    "Eat your dinner. Every bite."

epitrope
 	
(eh PIH trope)
	seemingly allowing the audience to make a judgment of its own; from "to yield" (Greek)
	
	Examples:
	
	    "He that is unjust, let him be unjust still: and he which is filthy, let him be filthy still: and he that is righteous, let him be righteous still: and he that is holy, let him be holy still." (Revelation 22:11)
	    "You be the judge."
	    "Go ahead. Make my day." (*Sudden Impact*, 1983)

equivocation
 	
(ee kwiv oh KAY shun)
	using words that have double meaning and words that are used as qualifiers
	
	purpose is often to deceive the audience by telling it what it wants to hear
	
	Example:
	
	    To doubt the equivocation of the fiend
	    That lies like truth. "Fear not, till Birnam wood
	    Do come to Dunsinane," and now a wood
	    Comes toward Dunsinane.
	    (*Macbeth*, V.v, Shakespeare)

eristic (err ISS tik)	an argument for the sake of arguing; an argument that does not seek truth or agreement
ethos (EE thahs)	a speaker's bearing and authority; from "character" (Greek) one creates a sense of ethos by using audience-appropriate diction and by including an opponent's counter-arguments in addition to one's own arguments [*see also* kairos, logos, pathos]

eucharistia (yoo kah RISS tee uh)	a statement of almost inexpressible gratitude **Examples:** "Thank you, judge, for your patience. I don't know how I can repay you." "I can't thank you people enough for this award!"
eutrepismus (yoo truh PISS muss)	a figure of dividing and ordering one's points or assertions; from "well turning" (Greek) also referred to as **enumeration** **Examples:** "I'm not going to ask her out because (a) her friends would make fun of me, (b) she has a car, and I don't, and (c) her boyfriend would kill me." I am enjoin'd by oath to observe three things: First, never to unfold to any one Which casket 'twas I chose; next, if I fail Of the right casket, never in my life To woo a maid in way of marriage: Lastly, If I do fail in fortune of my choice, Immediately to leave you and be gone. (*Merchant of Venice*, II.ix, Shakespeare)
evidence	support for a claim; proof of an assertion Types of evidence: **empirical evidence**—research or support based on direct or indirect observation **testimonial evidence**—support based on the personal affirmations by experts and other authorities **anecdotal evidence**—support based on hearsay or unverifiable stories
exclamatio (eks klahm AH tee oh)	a rhetorical expression with passion and emotion in exclamation form **Examples:** "O judgment! thou art fled to brutish beasts" (*Julius Caesar*, III.ii, Shakespeare) "O, God! a beast, that wants discourse of reason, / Would have mourn'd longer" (*Hamlet*, I.ii, Shakespeare)

excursus

(EK skur sis)

a lengthy digression

---

exergasia

(eks er GAS ee uh)

the repetition of the same idea in successive clauses, but in different words or mode of delivery; from "working out" (Greek)

Examples:

> "He gathereth the waters of the sea together as an heap: He layeth up the depth in storehouses." (Psalms 33:7)

> "Blessed is the man that walketh not in the counsel of the ungodly, nor standeth in the way of sinners, nor sitteth in the seat of the scornful." (Psalms 1:1)

---

extemporaneous

(eks temp uh RAY nee us)

an oral presentation or performance presented with little or no preparation

---

exuscitatio

(eks uss sih TAH tee oh)

a call to action using impassioned rhetorical questions; from "to awaken" (Greek)

Examples:

> "Are we going to stand by and let the administration take away our rights? Are we going to play servant to their master? Is any one of you afraid to take the fight to them?"

---

false dilemma

alternatives presented as an **either/or fallacy**

includes **alliosis,** which contains two alternatives presented in a parallel structure of essentially equal lengths (**isocolon**)

Examples:

> "Either you can clean your room, or you can stay home this weekend."

> "Either we stand together or we die together."

> "If you don't vote for this proposition, you will ruin this country!"

hasty generalization	a logical fallacy that incorrectly draws a conclusion from an insufficiently representative source

Examples:

> "I saw a teenager drive fast today; therefore, all teenagers are dangerous drivers."
>
> "My teacher last year punished the class all of the time; therefore, teachers are mean."

holophrasis (huh LOFF ruh sis)	expressing an idea of a phrase or sentence with one word

Examples:

> "Lame!"
>
> "Change"

hypophora (hahy POH fore uh)	rhetorical figure in which the speaker asks and then immediately answers his or her own questions

also referred to as a **rhetorical fragment**, **anthypophora** (AN thee POH FORE ah), or **rogatio** (roh GAH tee oh)

Examples:

> "When the enemy struck on that June day of 1950, what did America do? It did what it always has done in all its times of peril. It appealed to the heroism of its youth." ("I Shall Go to Korea," Dwight D. Eisenhower, 1952)
>
> "'But there are only three hundred of us,' you object. Three hundred, yes, but men, but armed, but Spartans, but at Thermoplyae: I have never seen three hundred so numerous." (Seneca)

ignoratio elenchi (ig noh ROT ee oh ey LEN chee)	inadvertently presenting an irrelevant argument or supporting the wrong conclusion

Examples:

> "Jennifer is going to be a great actress—she loves to watch TV."
>
> "Mark Jones should be elected to the U.S. Senate because he's been wanting to be a politician all of his life."

[*see also* red herring]

indignatio

(in dig NOT ee oh)

a rebuke caused by great indignation; from "displeasure" (Latin)

also referred to as **aganactesis** (AG an ak TEE sis) and is a type of **ecphonesis** (ek foh NEE sis), an emotional exclamation)

Examples:

> "What you have done is beyond reproach! I don't know how your mother and I will ever trust you again!"
>
> "A bloody deed! almost as bad, good mother, / As kill a king, and marry with his brother." (*Hamlet*, III.iv, Shakespeare)

[*see also* paeanismus]

induction

with respect to logic, the process of using specific instances to prove a premise or conclusion

induction also refers to an introductory element or event that precedes the main action of a narrative or play (a **prelude**)

Example:

> "I have scored well on every one of Ms. Smith's history tests so far. Therefore, I believe I will score well on her test tomorrow."

[*see also* deduction]

innuendo

(in yoo EN doh)

a subtle or indirect (usually negative) suggestion about something or someone

Example:

> "Let me tell you, Cassius, you yourself / Are much condemn'd to have an itching palm;" (*Julius Caesar*, IV.iii, Shakespeare)

[*see also* double entendre, intimation]

inopinatum

(in oh pih NAY tum)

a rhetorical expression of disbelief; from "powerless" (Latin)

Examples:

> "I can't imagine why you thought I would go along with you on that!"
>
> "Did you really think that I would believe you?"

[*see also* aporia, erotema, rhetorical question]

intimation

(in tuh MAY shun)

a subtle or indirect hint or suggestion

[*see also* innuendo]

---

invective

(in VEK tiv)

a harsh, scathing denunciation against a person or institution

also referred to as a **harangue** (huh RANG) or a **tirade** (TAHY raid)

Example:

> For Brutus, as you know, was Caesar's angel:
> Judge, O you gods, how dearly Caesar loved him!
> This was the most unkindest cut of all;
> For when the noble Caesar saw him stab,
> Ingratitude, more strong than traitors' arms,
> Quite vanquished him: then burst his mighty heart;
> (*Julius Caesar*, III.ii, Shakespeare)

[*see also* polemic]

---

ipse dixit

(ip SEE DIK sit)

a subjective, dogmatic assertion with no supporting evidence

---

jingoism

(JING oh izm)

bombastic language befitting extreme patriotism, including, in some instances, fanaticism and belligerence

---

kairos

(KAHY rohs)

speaking at an opportune time and with appropriate rhetorical sensitivity; from "at the right moment" (Greek)

[*see also* ethos, logos, pathos, rhetorical sensitivity]

leptologia (lep toh LOH jee uh)	using intentionally ambiguous or deceitful language to evade the true issue at hand; also refers to the criticism of minor points with no intention of resolving the core issue also referred to as **quibbling** **Example:** "I didn't explicitly say for you to cheat on the test; I simply told you to use every opportunity that presented itself." [*see also* equivocation]
logic	using reason as part of a formal argument; from "reason" (Greek) logic relies on establishing an argument, having sound reasoning, and providing supporting evidence
logical fallacy	an error in logic, leading to a false conclusion
logos (LOH gahs)	quality of reason or logic in an argument; from "reason" (Greek) logos is the essential nature of logic [*see also* ethos, kairos, pathos]
Loki's wager (LOH keez WAY jurr)	a logical fallacy by which a concept is stated to be impossible to define and therefore impossible to resolve derives from the Norse legend of Loki, the trickster god **Example:** "There's really not a definition of what a good curfew time is, so I really shouldn't have a curfew at all."
martyria (mar TEER ee ah)	a logical fallacy by which an assertion is supported by referring to one's own experience **Examples:** "I know that the administration is going to change programs because in my thirty years of teaching, they have never stayed with one program for long." "That can't be; I've never heard anything like that in my life!"

mempsis (memp SIS *or* MEMP sis)	a statement of reproach; from "blame" (Greek) **Example:** "Et tu, Brute?" (*Julius Caesar,* III.i, Shakespeare) "This is, quite simply, your worst behavior on this trip by far."
merism (MEH rizm)	a statement that lists parts to represent a whole **Examples:** "In the beginning God created the **heaven** and the **earth**." (Genesis 1:1) [the entire universe] "Thou shalt not be afraid for the **terror by night**; nor for the **arrow that flieth by day**;" (Psalms 91:5) [dangers present everyday]
metabasis (meh TAH buh sis)	a statement that summarizes that which has already been said and previews what will be said next **Example:** "I have shown you the graphs showing the number of widgets we sold last year, and now I want to explain to you how we can sell more widgets this year." [*see also* preacher's method]
metalepsis (met uh LEP sis)	a figure of speech in which a remote association is made; as critic Harold Bloom notes, "a metonymy of a metonymy" **Example:** The darkness drops again but now I know That twenty centuries of stony sleep Were vexed to nightmare by a **rocking cradle**, And what rough beast, its hour come round at last, Slouches towards **Bethlehem** to be born? ("The Second Coming," William Butler Yeats)
metanoia (met ah NOY ah)	retracting a statement to say it in a more effective way **Example:** "And if I am still far from the goal, the fault is my own for not paying heed to the reminders--nay, the virtual directions--which I have had from above." (*Meditations*, Marcus Aurelius)

metastasis (muh TASS tuh sis)	a sudden change of subject

Example:

> Q: "Do you support government deregulation?"
>
> A: "As mayor, I fought for lower taxes and more public services."

[*see also* red herring]

Monroe's Motivated Sequence

an organizational pattern for persuasive speeches; comprised of the following five elements:

1. **Attention**: Grab the attention of one's audience

2. **Need**: Specify the problem that needs solving

3. **Satisfy**: Articulate solutions to the problem

4. **Visualization**: Help the audience visualize what will (or will not) happen with adoption of the proposed solutions

5. **Action**: Give the audience a call to action

No true Scotsman

a logical fallacy articulated by Antony Flew in the late 20th century in which a claim cannot be disproven, no matter what evidence or reasoning is presented to the contrary

Example:

> "Imagine Hamish McDonald, a Scotsman, sitting down with his Glasgow Morning Herald and seeing an article about how the 'Brighton Sex Maniac Strikes Again.' Hamish is shocked and declares that 'No Scotsman would do such a thing.' The next day he sits down to read his Glasgow Morning Herald again and this time finds an article about an Aberdeen man whose brutal actions make the Brighton sex maniac seem almost gentlemanly. This fact shows that Hamish was wrong in his opinion but is he going to admit this? Not likely. This time he says, 'No true Scotsman would do such a thing.'" (*Thinking about Thinking*, Antony Flew)

[*see also* circular reasoning, dogma]

---

non sequitur

(nahn SEK kwuh turr)

a statement that does not logically follow the preceding argument or assertion

Example:

> "Students should be allowed to have cell phones on campus because cell phones are really cheap right now."

Occam's Razor (AHK umz RAY zurr)	a principle attributed to William of Ockham of the 14th century, who suggested that the best decision is one that requires no more variables than necessary; that is, when one has two competing theories or explanations that reach the same conclusion, the simpler one is the better also spelled **Ockham's Razor**
optatio (opp TAH tee oh)	an expressed fervent wish or desire **Examples:** "Judge, I hope that you see the damaging impacts of the affirmative's plan." "Why, look you, how you storm! / I would be friends with you and have your love," (*The Merchant of Venice*, I.iii, Shakespeare)
oratory (ORE uh tore ee)	the art and delivery of formal public speaking or a formal public speech; from "to speak" (Latin)
paeanismus (pay ah NISS mus)	an exclamation of joy; from "hymn" (Greek) a type of **ecphonesis** (ek foh NEE sis), an emotional exclamation **Example:** "Why, 'tis a loving and a fair reply" (*Hamlet*, I.ii, Shakespeare) [*see also* indignatio]
paradiastole (pah rah dahy ASS toh lee)	referring to someone's weakness or disadvantage in a positive way so as to appease or flatter **Examples:** "I know many people say you're cocky; I say you're confident." "It doesn't matter that you didn't finish the race; at least you tried, and that's more than those who didn't could say."
paradigm (PAIR uh dime)	an argument from example; a model **Example:** "The last person who came out of her office was crying; I suggest you prepare for the worst!"

paraenesis

(pah RANE ih sis)

a warning of impending doom; from "exhortation" (Greek)

Examples:

> "I heard this test is impossible; we're all going to fail."
> "We're all going to die!"

---

paralipsis

(pair uh LIP sis)

declaring something by way of feigned omission; from "to leave to the side" (Greek)

also referred to as **cataphasis** (kah TAFF ah sis), **parasiopesis** (pair uh SYE oh PEE sis), **praeteritio** (pray TARE ih toh), or **occupatio** (okk yoo PAHT ee oh)

taken to an extreme by including explicit detail, paralipsis becomes **proslepsis** (prohs LEEP sis)

Examples:

> "I don't want to focus on my opponent's lack of civic responsibility. Instead, I want to focus on the issues."
> "I will not make age an issue in this campaign. I'm not going to exploit for political purposes my opponent's youth and inexperience." (Ronald Reagan, who was 73 years old at the time, addressing his 56-year-old opponent, Walter Mondale, during the 1984 Presidential Debate)

[*see also* apophasis]

---

parelcon

(pah RELL kahn)

the use of two words where one suffices or any words when none is needed; from "to draw out" (Greek)

also used as a synonym for **paragoge**

Examples:

> "He is, **like**, the only person qualified for the job."
> "The president is, **you know**, elected every four years."
> "She is a **chatty, talkative** person."

---

pareuresis

(par yoor REE sis)

a convincing, but not altogether valid, excuse; from "pretense" (Greek)

Example:

> "My computer crashed, so I couldn't finish the assignment on time."

paromologia (par oh moh LOH jee uh)	conceding a point to make a better one; from "a partial agreement" (Greek) also referred to as **synchoresis** (sin koh REE sis) or **concessio** (kon SESS ee oh)

Examples:

"The other candidate makes a good point concerning the reduction of taxes, but he doesn't go far enough."

"I may have had a reckless youth, but I have learned from my mistakes and am a better person for it."

"True! —nervous – very, very dreadfully nervous I had been and am; but why will you say that I am mad? The disease has sharpened my senses – not destroyed – not dulled them." ("The Tell-Tale Heart," Edgar Allan Poe)

parrhesia (puh RAY zhuh)	to speak offensively or candidly but with apologies or with a request for permission; from "beyond speech" (Greek)

Examples:

"I don't want to offend anybody, but I think anyone who would vote for that person is a moron."

"I could be wrong, but didn't you make a mistake on your analysis?"

pathos (PAY thahs *or* PAY thohs)	a speaker's appeal to emotion in a rhetorical argument; the quality of a work to arouse pity, sorrow, or tenderness in the audience or reader; from "emotion" or "passion" (Greek) [*see also* ethos, kairos, logos]

perclusio (purr CLOO see oh)	a threat

Examples:

"You say something about my family one more time, and I'm going to punch your lights out."

"Look at me like that again, and you will looking with a black eye tomorrow."

periergia (per ee EHR jee uh)	simple verbosity or the overuse of figures of speech

Example from literature:

> Full thirty times hath Phoebus' cart gone round
> Neptune's salt wash and Tellus' orbed ground,
> And thirty dozen moons with borrow'd sheen
> About the world have times twelve thirties been,
> Since love our hearts and Hymen did our hands
> Unite commutual in most sacred bands.
> (*Hamlet*, III.ii, Shakespeare)

Example in rhetoric:

> "Your last contention, the point at which you were discussing the prior points, must be considered before any subsequent points or contentions can be discussed."

[*see also* circumlocution]

post hoc fallacy (post HOK FAL uh see)	a fallacy that incorrectly attributes one event as the cause of a second event because of close proximity in time between the two events

literally ***post hoc, ergo propter hoc*** "after this, therefore because of this" (Greek)

The best test for the post hoc fallacy is to ask the question, "Would the second event have occurred if the first had not occurred?"

preacher's method	a basic organizational formula for an expository composition or presentation:

1. tell the audience what points will be covered
2. cover the points
3. tell the audience what points were covered

procatalepsis (pro KAH tah LEP sis)	a rhetorical strategy in which the speaker raises objections to his or her own contention but then immediately answers them sometimes referred to as **prolepsis** (pro LEP sis)

Examples:

> "Some teenagers cannot be trusted with credit cards, but that should not keep all teenagers from using them."

> "It is again objected, as a very absurd, ridiculous custom....But this objection is, I think, a little unworthy so refined an age as ours. Let us argue this matter calmly." ("A Modest Proposal," Jonathan Swift)

proecthesis (proh EK thee sis)	validating one's position at the conclusion of an argument by giving a reason for one's position or actions

Examples:

> "I had to support this bill because it was the right action at the right time."

> "I will have mercy, and not sacrifice: for I am not come to call the righteous, but sinners to repentance." (Matthew 9:13)

propaganda (prop uh GAN duh)	media that have the sole purpose to persuade people to support a particular religious or political cause

pysma (PIHS mah)	the asking of multiple rhetorical questions in rapid succession; can be used to confuse or pester

Example:

> "How can you be so careless? What were you thinking? Do you only think about yourself? Do you know how much a replacement will cost? Do you have any idea?"

ratiocinatio (RAH tih oh cin AH tee oh)	reasoning through questioning; sometimes by self-questioning

Examples:

> "If I wanted to steal from you, wouldn't I have already done it?"
> "Why don't I trust you? Probably because you've lied to me before."

red herring (red HARE ing)	a diversion or non sequitur meant to move an argument or discussion in a different direction **Example:** "My opponent would like for you to think the economic picture is dismal, but I disagree. My family has a tradition of serving our community and finding the best in others."
reductio ad absurdum (ree duk TEE oh ab SUR dum)	making the conclusion that an argument's result would be ridiculous; taking an argument to an extreme in order to discredit it; from "reducing to absurdity" (Latin) **Example:** "Well, we can't guarantee complete protection from all rodents unless you want me to put a cement tent around your house." [*see also* slippery slope]
repartee (reh par TAY)	a quick, often witty, retort; from "quick remark" (French) **Example:** Dan Quayle: "I have as much experience in the Congress as Jack Kennedy did when he sought the presidency...." Lloyd Bentsen: "Senator, I served with Jack Kennedy: I knew Jack Kennedy; Jack Kennedy was a friend of mine. Senator, you're no Jack Kennedy." (1988 Vice Presidential Debate)

rhetoric (RET uh rik)	the art of effective speaking and writing, particularly with respect to persuasion there are five canons of rhetoric:

- **Invention**—finding something to say
- **Arrangement**—putting those things in order (dispositio)
- **Style**—the manner in which those things are said
- **Memory**—storing material for use in rhetoric
- **Delivery**—delivering the oratory

also, Aristotle enumerated three types of rhetoric:

- **demonstrative rhetoric** (also referred to as **epideitic** (ep ih dee IK tik) refers to the rhetoric used for ceremonies, festivals, celebrations, and funerals
- **forensic rhetoric** refers to rhetoric used for legal proceedings
- **deliberative rhetoric** refers to rhetoric used for politics and legislation

a notable development in the study of contemporary rhetoric is the analysis of images and visual design, otherwise known as **visual rhetoric**

[*see also* dispositio, stasis, topos]

rhetorical question (ruh TORE ih kull KWES chun)	a question posed that requires no answer, nor is one expected; used solely for rhetorical effect also referred to as **erotesis** (eh roh TEE sis) or **erotema** (eh roh TEM ah)

Example:

"How much do we have to endure before we act?"

[*see also* pysma]

rhetorical sensitivity

(ruh TORE ih kull sin suh TIV uh tee)

the speaker's understanding of and empathy with his or her audience

a consciousness of how a speaker's choices of topic, diction, and delivery style will impact the audience's impression of the speaker and the message

Example:

Positive rhetorical sensitivity
"I know you are all busy, so I'm going to go through this presentation fast and highlight the key points."

Poor rhetorical sensitivity
"What I'm going to cover will be over your head, but do your best to keep up."

[*see also* ethos, kairos]

rodomontade

(rod oh mon TOD)

a pretentious oration of boasting or self-aggrandizement

Rogerian Model of Argumentation

(roh ZHAIR ee un)

a model of argumentation, developed by psychologist Carl Rogers, that seeks to find common ground between speaker and audience and relies more on pathos and ethos rather than logos

contains the following elements:

- a brief definition of the problem in objective language

- a neutral statement of the opposition's point of view and reasoning for that point of view

- a neutral statement of the speaker's point of view and reasoning for that point of view

- a statement of what the positions have in common and what values they share

- a statement of position that seeks a compromise of both positions or another position that benefits both parties

[*see also* Aristotelian Model of Argumentation, Toulmin Model of Argumentation]

segue (SEG way)	a smooth transition from one point to another

skotison (SKOH tih son)	intentionally ambiguous speech or code with the purpose to confuse; from "to darken" (Greek) often used as an exclusive means of communicating within an group, such as the military **Examples:** "FUBAR" (fouled up beyond all recognition) "SNAFU" (situation normal: all fouled up)

slippery slope	a logical fallacy that proposes one consequence will invariably lead to a second (unwanted) consequence **Examples:** "Give teenagers an inch, and they'll take a mile!" "If we vote for this candidate, he will take away our guns."

speech act theory	a theory, set forth by J.L. Austin, that explains how what someone says actually constitutes an act the delivery of what the speaker is seeking to do in an oratory (the intended meaning) is the **illocutionary act** the expression or utterance of the speech act (the actual meaning) is the **locutionary act** the actual effect of the speech act is the **perlocutionary act** **Example:** **locutionary act**: "You're in my way." **illocutionary act**: "*I need to get to the train on time or let the person know that he is simply moving too slowly.*" **perlocutionary act**: "*I convinced the person to get out of the way.*"

Socratic dialogue

(so KRAT ik DAHY uh log)

a teaching method meant to draw out inferences and interpretations through constant questioning; popularized by the ancient Greek philosopher Socrates

Example:

Q: "What is the meaning of life?"
A: "To serve a higher purpose."
Q: "And what is that purpose?"
A: "To help others."
Q: "And how does that serve a higher purpose?"
and so on....

solecism

(SOH lih sizm)

a mistake in grammar or usage; intentional use may be poetic license

Examples:

"This argument is between you and I."
"The award should go to **whom** is fastest in the race."
"I will vote on this bill **irregardless** of what my colleagues do."

sophia

(soh FEE uh *or* SOH fee uh)

what the ancient Greek philosopher Aristotle termed as innate wisdom; it is theoretical, philosophical thinking and can be contrasted with **phronesis** (froh NEE sis), which is practical thinking, better known as "street smarts"

sprezzatura

(SPRET suh turr uh)

a natural, seemingly effortless presentation or performance; the art of making a difficult task seem easy

originated from Baldesar Castiglione's *The Book of the Courtier*

[*see also* ethos]

stasis (STAY sis)	the questions one asks to arrive at the point of assertion (**contention**); from "to take a stand" (Greek) there are four stases from classical rhetorical teachings: • **Conjecture**—asking the question, "does the thing at issue exist?" • **Definition**—asking the question, "what is at issue?" • **Quality**—asking the question, "is the issue good or bad?" • **Procedure**—asking the question, "is this the right time and place to address this issue?" [*see also* rhetoric]

stipulative definition (STIP yoo luh tiv)	an agreed upon definition for the sake of an argument **Examples:** "In this debate, when we talk about alternative fuels, we will both agree that the term *alternative fuels* means any non-petroleum-based fuels."

straw man	straw man fallacies build up a simplified and illogical or damaged assertion that one presents as something that one's opposition supports or represents; then one proceeds to attack this idea and, thus, one's opponent **Example:** "While my opponent would like to empty our prisons of serial killers and coddle pedophiles, I hold to the sacred principle of an eye for an eye."

syllogism (SILL oh jizm)	a rhetorical discourse in which certain premises have been made and something other than these premises follows as a result

In a syllogism, the primary premise is a universal general statement. The secondary premise may also be universal or particular so that from these premises it is possible to deduce a valid conclusion; from "reckoning together" (Greek)

Examples:

> Everything that lives, moves (primary premise)
> No mountain moves (secondary premise)
> Therefore, no mountain lives (conclusion)

> SIEGFRIED: How do I know you're not Control?
>
> AGENT 86: If I were from Control, you'd already be dead.
>
> SIEGFRIED: If you were Control, you'd already be dead.
>
> AGENT 86: Well, neither of us is dead, so I'm obviously not from Control.

> (*Get Smart*, 2008)

[*see also* enthymeme]

syncrisis (SIN krih sis)	a comparison of opposites in parallel form; from "combination" (Greek)

Examples:

> "You yearned for change, but you voted for the status quo."
> "It's not a matter of science; it's a matter of faith."

[*see also* antithesis]

topos (TOE pohs)	in rhetoric, categories or relationships among ideas, as well as ways in which those ideas will be developed and discussed; from "a place" (Greek)

also, a device or convention in a literary work

the plural is **topoi** (TOH poi)

Toulmin Model of Argumentation

(TOHL min)

a process of reasoning, developed by philosopher Stephen Toulmin, that moves from fact or perceived fact (datum) to claim

the model progresses in the following manner:

- **Claim** (the intended assertion)
- **Datum** (reason or fact for the claim; evidence)
- **Warrant** (support for the datum)
- **Backing** (further support for the warrant)
- **Qualifier** (a limitation of the claim)
- **Rebuttal** (possible exceptions to the claim)

Example:

Jim Robbins probably votes Republican because he lives in Northwest Arkansas. You see, according to the *Arkansas Democrat-Gazette*, most of the voters in the northwestern region of Arkansas vote Republican. At the very least, he probably votes Republican at least most of the time.

Claim (Jim Robbins probably votes Republican)

Datum (Jim Robbins lives in Northwest Arkansas)

Warrant (most of the voters in the northwestern region of Arkansas vote Republican)

Backing (according to the *Democrat-Gazette*)

Qualifier (words such as *most*, *probably*)

Rebuttal (at least most of the time)

[*see also* Aristotelian Model of Argumentation, Rogerian Model of Argumentation]

treppenwitz

(trepp in VITZ)

the repartee or rhetorically powerful reply that only becomes apparent after the debate; the brilliant comeback one has after a discussion or debate is well over; from "staircase wit" (German)

also referred to as **espirit d'escalier** (ess SPREE duh SKAL yay)

anacoluthon (an uh kuh LOO thahn)	a sudden shift in the implied grammatical sequence within a sentence; often used stylistically; from "not marching together" (Greek)

Examples:

"Had ye been there—for what could that have done?" (*Lycidas*, John Milton)

"If thou beest he; But O how fall'n! how chang'd / From him" (*Paradise Lost*, Book I, John Milton)

anadiplosis (an uh dahy PLOH sis)	repetition of a word or phrase at the end of one line or clause and the beginning of the next line or clause

Examples:

"As thou being **mine**, **mine** is thy good report." ("Sonnet 36," Shakespeare)

"Fear leads to **anger**. **Anger** leads to **hate**. **Hate** leads to suffering." (*Star Wars: The Phantom Menace*, 1999)

[*see also* conduplicatio]

anaphora (an NAFF or uh)	the repetition of the same word or phrase at the beginning of successive lines or clauses

Examples:

"**We shall fight** on the beaches, **we shall fight** on the landing-grounds, **we shall fight** in the fields and in the streets, **we shall fight** in the hills." (Winston Churchill)

"To everything there is a season, and a time for every purpose under the heavens. **A time to** be born, and **a time to** die; **a time to** plant, and **a time to** reap; **a time to** kill, and **a time to** heal; **a time to** tear down, and **a time to** build; **a time to** weep, and **a time** to laugh; **a time to** mourn and **a time to** dance." (Ecclesiastes 3:1)

"**I haven't heard how his policy** on Iran is going to be different than George Bush's. **I haven't heard how his policy** with Israel will be different than George Bush's. **I haven't heard how his policy** on Afghanistan will be different than George Bush's. **I haven't heard how his policy** in Pakistan will be different than George Bush's." (Vice Presidential Debate, Joe Biden, 2008)

[*see also* epistrophe]

anapodoton

(AN uh POH doh tahn)

a rhetorical figure in which the subordinate clause, which is present, implies the meaning of the main clause, which is not present; from "leaving out the main clause" (Greek)

Examples:

> "When you're ready."
>
> "Because people care about the economy!"

[*see also* ellipsis]

anastrophe

(an ASS truh fee)

a rhetorical figure involving a reversal of word order to make a point

also referred to as **inversion** or **hyperbaton**

Example:

> "This is the sort of English up with which I will not put!"
>
> (Winston Churchill's reply to the rule that sentences should never end with prepositions)

antimetabole

(an tee muh TAH boh lee)

figure of speech in which two or more words are repeated in a successive clause, but in reverse order

a type of chiasmus

Examples:

> "All for one, and one for all." (*The Three Musketeers*, Alexandre Dumas)
>
> "Absence of evidence is not evidence of absence." (*The Demon-Haunted World*, Carl Sagan)

apposition

(app oh ZIH shun)

two adjacent expressions, the second of which serving as an explanation of the first

Examples:

> "Mr. Thibodeaux, a mysterious stranger to many, was never seen outside his home."
>
> "I would like for you to meet Mr. Stoll, my next-door neighbor."

asyndeton (uh SIN duh tahn)	intentional omission of conjunctions in clauses that would otherwise need them also referred to as **parataxis** (pair uh TAKS iss) **Example:** "I came; I saw; I conquered."(Julius Caesar) "If, as is the case, we feel responsibility, are ashamed, are frightened, at transgressing the voice of conscience, this implies that there is one to whom we are responsible, before whom we are ashamed, whose claims upon us we fear." (*Grammar of Assent*, John Henry Newman) [*see also* brachyology]

brachyology (bruh KILL uh jee)	the omission of conjunctions between individual words or an abbreviated (but well understood) phrase; from "short speech" (Greek) **Examples:** "Morning" for "Good morning" "Sup?" for "What's up?" (slang) "Woke, showered, ate—I'm ready for today!" [*see also* asyndeton]

balanced sentence	a sentence that contains phrases or clauses that are similar in length or syntax **Example:** "He maketh me to lie down in green pastures; he leadeth me beside the still waters." (Psalms 23:2)

centered sentence	a sentence in which the main clause is in the middle and is bounded on either side by subordinate constructions **Examples:** "Finally understanding the gravity of his crime, Martin decided to turn himself in, not concerned in the least by the consequences." "Having been raised on the farm, Susan had no problem with navigating the horse pasture, unlike her husband, who seemed to be having a bit more trouble."

chiasmus (kye AZZ muss)	two parallel phrases or clauses, the second of which being a reversal of the first; from "placing crosswise" (Greek) **Examples:** "Ask not what your country can do for you; ask what you can do for your country."("Inaugural Address," John F. Kennedy, 1961) "Now, women forget all those things they don't want to remember, and remember everything they don't want to forget." (*Their Eyes Were Watching God*, Zora Neale Hurston)
collocation	the conventional arrangement of adjoining words, respective to a particular language Examples: The word *pretty* is often used for an attractive woman ("pretty woman") but not for an attractive man ("handsome man"), and the converse is usually true also. [see also idiom]
complex sentence	a sentence made up of an independent clause and one or more dependent clauses **Examples:** "When I get to school, I'll finish my homework." "I'm going to stay in this class, although I am currently failing because I missed two big tests."
compound sentence	a sentence made up of two independent clauses **Examples:** "Janie wanted to watch television, but Martha wanted to go to the mall." "He is a very fast talker; he is also very articulate."
compound-complex sentence	a sentence made up of two or more independent clauses and one or more dependent clauses **Examples:** "He is the best candidate for this position, and because the country needs his experience, he will get the most votes this November." "Although I am ready for school, I have to wait on my sister, but she hasn't even woken up yet!"

conduplicatio

(kahn doo plee KAT ee oh)

the repetition of a key word from a previous sentence or phrase at the beginning of a successive sentence or phrase or clause

Examples:

"The strength of the **passions** will never be accepted as an excuse for complying with them; the **passions** were designed for subjection, and if a man suffers them to get the upper hand, he then betrays the liberty of his own soul." (Alexander Pope)

"This afternoon, in this room, I testified before the Office of Independent Council and the Grand Jury. I answered their **questions** truthfully, including **questions** about my private life -- **questions** no American citizen would ever want to answer." ("Address to the Nation," Bill Clinton, 1968)

[*see also* anadiplosis]

convoluted sentence

a sentence in which the main clause is split by one or more subordinate constructions

Examples:

"Mr. Mayapple, for all of his faults, is still a nice man."

"The tomato, contrary to popular belief, is a fruit, not a vegetable."

cumulative sentence

(KYOOM yuh luh tiv)

an independent clause followed by a series of phrases or subordinate clauses, which build upon each other as elaboration, but are not necessary to make sense of the original clause

also referred to as a **loose sentence**

Example:

"We finally saw the movie after a stressful afternoon, tired but excited, ready to tell our friends all about the show."

dependent clause

a group of words that contains a subject and a predicate but does not express a complete thought

Examples:

"Although he went to the beach"

"Having a nagging doubt"

[*see also* independent clause]

diacope (dahy AH koh pee)	repetition interrupted by only an occasional word or phrase, usually for an emotional effect; from "a gash or cut" (Greek)

Examples:

"To the swinging and the ringing / Of the bells, bells, bells-- / Of the bells, bells, bells, bells" ("The Bells," Edgar Allan Poe)

"All lost! To prayers, to prayers! All lost!" (*The Tempest*, I.i, Shakespeare)

"Alone, alone, all all alone, / Alone on a wide wide sea" (*The Rime of the Ancient Mariner*, Part IV, Samuel Taylor Coleridge)

[*see also* epizeuxis]

diazeugma (dahy ah ZOOG muh)	a construction in which one subject has many verbs

Examples:

"Upon my touching him, **he** immediately **rose**, **purred** loudly, **rubbed** against my hand, and **appeared** delighted with my notice." ("The Black Cat," Edgar Allan Poe)

"Now he's ready: fastball, high, ball two. You can't blame a man for pushing just a little bit now. **Sandy backs off**, **mops** his forehead, **runs** his left index finger along his forehead, **dries** it off on his left pants leg. All the while Kuenn just waiting....Sandy into his windup, here's the pitch: Swung on and missed, a perfect game!" (Vin Scully, reporting a play-by-play of Sandy Koufax's perfect game in 1965)

[*see also* zeugma]

ellipsis (eh LIP sis)	intentional omission of words or phrases that are otherwise understood by context; also refers to a narrative device in which insignificant events are omitted from the story

Example:

"Jimmy lost three dollars, Emily two."

[*see also* anapodoton]

epanalepsis (eh puh nuh LEEP sis)	a syntactic structure in which a word or phrase at the beginning of a sentence or line of verse reappears at the end

Example:

"The king is dead, long live the king."

epanorthosis

(eh pih nor THOH sis)

an immediate clarification or qualification of a statement to better reflect the speaker's true intent or to make the statement more powerful

Examples:

"Give me chastity and continence, **but not yet**." (*Confessions*, St. Augustine)

"God bless **the King, (I mean the faith's defender!)** / God bless! (No harm in blessing) the Pretender." ("A Toast Intended to Allay the Violence of Party-Spirit," John Byrom)

"We have learned to fly. What prodigious changes are involved in that new accomplishment! Man has parted company with his trusty friend the horse and has sailed into the azure with the eagles, eagles being represented by the **infernal - I mean internal -combustion engine**." ("The Price of Greatness is Responsibility," Winston Churchill, 1943)

epergesis

(eh purr JEE sis)

a clarification by way of apposition

also spelled **epexegesis**

Examples:

"Your friends, that is, you in particular, are the nicest people I have met at this school."

"I'm willing to give you twenty bucks if you mow the yard, the front yard and the back yard, for me."

epistrophe

(eh PIHS truh fee)

the repetition of the same word or phrase at the ending of successive statements

also referred to as **antistrophe** (ann TISS troh fee)

Examples:

"In 1931, ten years ago, Japan invaded Manchukuo—**without warning**. In 1935, Italy invaded Ethiopia—**without warning**. In 1938, Hitler occupied Austria—**without warning**. In 1939, Hitler invaded Czechoslovakia—**without warning**. Later in 1939, Hitler invaded Poland—witho**ut warning**. And now Japan has attacked Malaya and Thailand—and the United States—**without warning**." ("Radio Address to the Nation," Franklin D. Roosevelt, 1941)

"I haven't heard how his policy on Iran is going to be **different than George Bush's**. I haven't heard how his policy with Israel will be **different than George Bush's**. I haven't heard how his policy on Afghanistan will be **different than George Bush's**. I haven't heard how his policy in Pakistan will be **different than George Bush's**." (Vice Presidential Debate, Joe Biden, 2008)

[*see also* anaphora]

epizeuxis

(ep uh ZOOK sis)

uninterrupted repetition of words or phrases for emphasis; from "to yoke" (Greek)

also referred to as **palilogia** (pal lih LOH jee uh)

Examples:

> "Words, words, words." (*Hamlet*, II.ii, Shakespeare)
>
> "Would you please please please please please please please stop talking?" ("Hills like White Elephants," Ernest Hemingway)

[*see also* diacope]

expletive

(EKS pluh tiv)

a single word or short phrase that is used to give emphasis or to fill out a sentence or line; from "filled up" (Latin)

also refers to unnecessary vulgar language used in a conversation, speech, or text

Examples:

> "No matter what you say, the yard was not, **in fact**, mowed this morning."
>
> "**Jiminy Cricket**, you always try to scare me!"
>
> "**Indeed**, the water I give him will become in him a spring of water welling up to eternal life." (John 4:14)

freight-train

several short independent clauses joined together by conjunctions to make a longer sequential statement

Examples:

> "And God said, 'Let the waters under the heaven be gathered together unto one place, and let the dry land appear:' and it was so." (Genesis 1:9)
>
> "Nick and his father got into the stern of the boat and the Indians shoved it off and one of them got in to row." ("Indian Camp," Ernest Hemingway)

[*see also* polysyndeton, stream of consciousness]

hendiadys (hen DAHY uh dis)	adding emphasis by using two nouns and a conjunction rather than a modifier and a noun; from "one thing by means of two" (Greek) **Examples:** "The kingdom and the power and the glory" rather than "powerful, glorious kingdom" (Matthew 6:13) "sound and fury" instead of "furious sound"(*Macbeth*, V.v, Shakespeare)
hypallage (hahy PAL uh jee)	the misalignment of word order for literary effect; from "exchange" (Greek) **Example:** "The **eye** / of man hath not **heard**, the **ear** of man hath not / **seen**, man's **hand** is not able to **taste**, his **tongue** / to **conceive**, nor his heart to report, what my dream / was." (*A Midsummer Night's Dream*, IV.i, Shakespeare) [*see also* transferred epithet]
hypozeugma (hahy poh ZOOG mah)	a series of words or parallel phrases followed by a shared verb (or other dependent word) **Examples:** "Friends, Romans, Countrymen, lend me your ears" (*Julius Caesar*, III.ii, Shakespeare) "The men in the towers, the women in the field, the children at the creek, all who are our countrymen, want nothing less than peace." [*see also* mesozeugma, prozeugma, zeugma]
hypozeuxis (hahy poh ZOOK sis)	a series of words or parallel clauses having an independent predicate each **Examples:** "My mind's made up—I've called your father, and you're no longer welcome here." "Madam, the guests are come, supper served up, you / called, my young lady asked for, the nurse cursed in / the pantry, and every thing in extremity. I must / hence to wait; I beseech you, follow straight." (*Romeo and Juliet*, I.iii, Shakespeare) [*see also* zeugma]

hysterologia

(hiss turr oh LOH jee uh)

substituting a preposition with another word or inserting a phrase between a preposition and its object

Examples:

"Where **the heck** are you going?"

"Are you still going to**, remember, you weren't invited,** the party?"

hysteron proteron

(HISS turr ahn PROH turr ahn)

a figurative or rhetorical device in which the first statement occurs later in time than the second statement in order to give the first statement prominence; from "the last is the first" (Greek)

Examples:

"Let us die, and rush into the midst of the fray" (*The Aeneid,* Book II, Virgil)

"Masters, it is proved already / that you are little better than false knaves; and it /will go near to be thought so shortly." (*Much Ado About Nothing,* IV.iv, Shakespeare)

independent clause

a group of words with a subject and a predicate and expresses a complete thought; a sentence must contain at least one independent clause

[*see also* dependent clause]

inverted syntax

involves constructing a sentence so the predicate comes before the subject; often used to create an emphatic or rhythmic effect

Example:

"At night *appear* the *raccoons.*"

[The subject (*raccoons*) appears after the predicate (*appear*).]

isocolon

(ahy soh KOH lahn)

a series of words, phrases, or clauses having similar syntax and length; from "equal member" (Greek)

Examples:

"Veni, vedi, vici" (Julius Caesar)

"I speak Spanish to God, Italian to women, French to men, and German to my horse." (Charles V)

juxtaposition

(JUKS tuh poh zish un)

the placement of contrasting ideas side by side

Example:

> "The apparition of these faces in the crowd:/Petals on a wet, black bough." ("In a Station of the Metro," Ezra Pound)

[*see also* antithesis]

---

mesodiplosis

(meh soh dip LOH sis)

the repetition of words or phrases in the middle of successive lines or clauses

Example:

> "We are perplexed, **but not** in despair; persecuted, **but not** forsaken; cast down, **but not** destroyed." (2 Corinthians 4:8)

---

mesozeugma

(may soh ZOOG mah)

a series of words or phrases split by a shared verb

Examples:

> "Your actions have been unconscionable, and his silence!"
> "My love could not be stronger, nor my dedication."

[*see also* hypozeugma, prozeugma, zeugma]

---

monepic

(muh NEP ik)

refers to a single word or a one-word sentence

Examples:

> "Run!"
> "His speech is monepic. These words consist of substantives, such as *mamma, nurse, milk*, and so forth." (*Popular Science*: "Studies of Childhood," James Sully)

---

natural syntax

involves constructing a sentence so the subject precedes the predicate

Example:

> "*Raccoons appear* at night."
> [The subject (*Raccoons*) appears before the predicate (*appear*).]

negative-positive

a sentence that begins with a negative statement and is followed by an affirming statement to the contrary

Examples:

"I don't like peanut butter, but I love jelly."

"Mankind cannot understand all of the secrets of the universe, yet we can still admire the beauty of the heavens."

[*see also* positive-negative]

---

parallel structure

clauses or phrases with similar grammatical structure, syntax, and length

often referred to as **parallelism** or **parison**

Example:

"He loved swimming, running, and hiking."

---

parenthetical

the insertion of a explanatory (or qualifying) word, phrase, or clause in a position that breaks the normal flow of the sentence and is enclosed within parenthesis marks

Example:

"One day in class we got off the subject (as often happens with over-worked, sleep-deprived juniors) and began to discuss the literature of Dr. Seuss."

---

periodic sentence

(peer ee ODD ik)

phrases or subordinate clauses followed by the main, independent clause; a sentence that is only grammatically complete and coherent at its end

Examples:

"No man of common humanity, no man who had any value for his character, could be capable of it." (*Pride and Prejudice*, Jane Austen)

---

ploce (PLOH kee *or* PLOH see)	the repetition of words in close (but not adjacent) proximity for the purpose of emphasis; from "to braid" (Greek) not to be confused with **epizeuxis**, which features the immediate repetition of words for emphasis also spelled **ploche**

Example:

> Which All from Nothing get, from Nothing, All:
> Hath All on Nothing set, lets Nothing fall.
> Gave All to nothing Man indeed, whereby
> Through nothing man all might him Glorify.
> ("The Preface," Edward Taylor)

> "Why wilt thou sleep the sleep of death, / And close her from thy ancient walls?" ("Jerusalem: To the Christians," William Blake)

> "Make war upon themselves; blood against blood, / Self against self" (*Richard III*, II.iv, Shakespeare)

[*see also* antistasis, diacope, epanalepsis, polyptoton, symploce]

polyptoton (poh LIP toh tahn)	a repetition of words from the same root of or the same word used as a different part of speech; from "many falling" (Greek)

Examples:

> "Love is not love / Which alters when it alteration finds, / Or bends with the remover to remove" ("Sonnet 116," Shakespeare)

> "Let me assert my firm belief that the only thing we have to fear is fear itself." ("Inaugural Address," Franklin D. Roosevelt, 1933)

polysyndeton (PAH lee sin duh TAHN)	intentional use of conjunctions to create a rhythmic flow or emphasis also referred to as **hypotaxis**

Examples:

> "The cause of the attitude was **not** ignorance, **not** apathy, **not** rejection, **but** hopelessness."

> "I willed myself to stay awake, **but** the rain was so soft **and** the room was so warm **and** his voice was so deep **and** his knee was so snug that I slept." (*To Kill a Mockingbird*, Harper Lee)

positive-negative	a sentence that begins with a positive statement and is followed by a statement to the contrary

Examples:

> "I'm going to ask Mary to the dance, but she will probably tell me no."
>
> "The beach is a wonderful place to relax, yet one has to be careful of sharks."

[*see also* negative-positive]

prozeugma (proh ZOOG mah)	a series of clauses in which successive clauses omit the verb that is implied from the first clause

Example:

> "His actions have denied me my liberty, his policies my quest for freedom, his rhetoric my supporters."

[*see also* hypozeugma, mesozeugma, zeugma]

repetition	a device that incorporates multiple uses of a sound, letter, word, phrase, or other literary or grammatical element for emphasis

Example:

> ". . . government of the people, by the people, for the people, shall not perish from the earth." ("The Gettysburg Address," 1963, Abraham Lincoln)

rhopalic (roh PAL ik)	a sentence or line of verse in which each successive word contains one more syllable or letter; from "club shaped" (Greek)

Examples:

> "Feeling unhappy, they made ready to depart for the next table, but their sufferings were not over, for Soapy fired off a rhopalic sentence, that is, one in which each word is one letter longer than the word that precedes it: 'I am the only dummy player, perhaps, planning maneuvers calculated brilliantly, nevertheless outstandingly pachydermatous, notwithstanding unconstitutional unprofessionalism.'" (Alan Truscott, *New York Times*, 1986)
>
> "She wore green jewels privily, admiring bantering gentrified celebrities."

run-on sentence	two or more independent clauses joined without proper punctuation

also referred to as a **fused sentence**

Examples:

"Studying is an important skill everybody knows that."

"I want to apply to that school, however, I don't have any scholarships."

[*see also* sentence fragment]

running style	a syntactic structure that mimics the thinking process in a raw, undeveloped, hurried manner

Example:

HAMLET	Now might I do it pat, now he is praying;
	And now I'll do't. And so he goes to heaven;
	And so am I revenged. That would be scann'd:
	A villain kills my father; and for that,
	I, his sole son, do this same villain send
	To heaven.

	To take him in the purging of his soul,
	When he is fit and season'd for his passage?
	No!
	Up, sword
	(*Hamlet*, III.iii, Shakespeare)

[*see also* stream of consciousness]

scesis onomaton (SKEE sis oh NOH muh tahn)	the repetition of words or phrases that are the same or essentially the same

Examples:

"Ah, sinful nation, a people laden with iniquity, a seed of evildoers, children that are corrupters: they have forsaken the Lord…" (Isaiah 1:4)

"For unto us a child is born, unto us a son is given; and the government shall be upon his shoulder; and his name shall be called Wonderful, Counselor, the mighty God, the everlasting Father, the Prince of Peace." (Isaiah 9:6)

segregating style a series of short, simple, yet varied, sentences or syntactical structures

Examples:

"I will decide when to leave. Not you. Not him. Me. I will decide."

"But I was never cured. The Thing remained there forever. Only moving West when I was thirteen got me away from that terror." (*Zen in the Art of Writing*, Ray Bradbury)

---

sentence fragment a group of words that is written as a sentence but cannot stand on its own as a complete thought

Examples:

"Because I heard the news."

"And went to the beach."

[*see also* run-on sentence]

---

sentence type refers to one of four functions of a sentence:

- **declarative sentences** simply make a statement and always end with a period (.)

- **imperative sentences** make a request or command and end with either a period or an exclamation point (. *or* !)

- **exclamatory sentences** express strong feeling or emphasis and always end with an exclamation point (!)

- **interrogative sentences** ask questions and always end with a question mark (?)

---

simple sentence an independent clause with no dependent clauses

Examples:

"My head hurts."

"Senator Smith has decided to run for office."

symploce

(SIM ploh see *or* SIM ploh kee)

a rhetorical structure combining **anaphora** and **epistrophe** (antistrophe); repeating a word or phrase at the beginning and end of successive phrases or clauses

Examples:

> "My brother need not be idealized, or enlarged in death beyond what he was in life, to be remembered simply as a good and decent man, who saw wrong and tried to right it, saw suffering and tried to heal it, saw war and tried to stop it." ("Eulogy for Robert Kennedy," Ted Kennedy, 1968)

> "**You don't want** the truth, **but you ask for it. You don't want** the hard talk, **but you ask for it. You don't want** the tough walk, **but you ask for it.**"

synchysis

(SIN kuh sis)

words formed in a confused pattern, often in an extreme form of inversion; from "to mix, to confuse" (Greek)

Example:

> "This time are you to assert your rights and obligations are you to fulfill."

synesis

(SIN uh sis)

a grammatical construction in which agreement is based on meaning rather than on actual number; from "to understand; to bring together" (Greek)

also referred to as **constructio ad sensum** (kahn STROOK tee oh ad SIN soom)

Example:

> "The committee made their decisions clear."

> [The pronoun *their* refers to the implied individual members of the committee rather than to the committee as a whole.]

syntactic fluency

(sin TAK tik FLOO in see)

the use of a variety of sentence structures in one's writing or speech

syntactic permutation

(sin TAK tik per myoo TAY shun)

sentences utilizing complex, varied styles of syntax, often causing difficulty for the reader

[*see also* circumlocution, stream of consciousness]

syntagmatic (sin tag MAT ik)	the horizontal relationship of words; that is, the connections that words in a phrase, clause, or sentence have to one another and thus, derive their meaning contrast with the vertical relationship of words, called **paradigmatic** (pare uh dig MAT ik), which represents the unspoken or unwritten words associated with those that are spoken and written and help to define their meaning (or conceptualization)
syntax	the way in which words and punctuation are put together to form phrases, clauses, and sentences, particularly to achieve a specific effect
triadic sentence	a sentence composed of three parts **Examples:** "Calvin Coolidge believed that the least government was the best government; he aspired to become the least President the country ever had; he attained his desire." (*The Aspirin Age*, Irving Stone)
tricolon	three parallel elements of the same length occurring together in a series **Example:** "Veni, vidi, vici." (Julius Caesar)

Elements of Language and Literature

abstract diction	language that denotes intangible concepts or ideas; abstract language refers to words that do not appeal to the reader's physical senses
	concrete diction, on the other hand, creates a mental picture and is something the observer (reader) can touch, smell, see, hear, or taste
	Example:
	"Susan and Kurt are having trouble in their relationship." [Here, the word *trouble* is abstract because it is not something an observer can see or experience in a tangible way.]
actant	one of six roles devised by A.J. Greimas that constitute basic fictional roles: Subject/Object; Sender/Receiver, Helper/Opponent
	the Sender sets forth what the Receiver is to do or want (object), thereby transforming the Receiver into the Subject; the Subject is then aided by the Helper and hindered by the Opponent
	human characters, non-human entities, and inanimate objects can all fulfill these roles
	Example:
	from *Harry Potter and the Chamber of Secrets*: **Sender**: Professor McGonagall (indirectly) **Receiver/Subject**: Harry Potter **Object**: Rescue Ginny Weasley **Helper**: Fawkes the Phoenix, the Sorting Hat **Opponent**: Basilisk, Voldemort (Tom Riddle)
	[*see also* narratology]
aesthetic (ess THET ik)	refers to the artistic beauty of a work, and what makes it so
	also spelled **esthetic**

aleatory

(AL ee uh tore ee *or* EY lee uh tore ee)

randomness of presentation in a literary work (e.g., stream of consciousness)

alter-ego

a character's separate identity or persona within a narrative

Examples:

> Macbeth, the brave and loyal Thane of Cawdor, is contrasted by his alter-ego, a plotting murderer willing to usurp the throne of Scotland (*Macbeth*, Shakespeare)

> The comic book characters Superman & Clark Kent (DC Comics) are two separate identities of the same person, as are Spider-Man and Peter Parker (Marvel Comics).

amanuensis

(uh man yoo EN sis)

a person who transcribes what is being dictated

Example:

> Alex Haley for Malcolm X (*The Autobiography of Malcolm X*)

ambiguity

(am buh GYOO uh tee)

an element of non-clarity or vagueness; may be intentional

the adjective form is **ambiguous** (am BIG yoo us)

anagram

(AN uh gram)

a word or name resulting from the transposition of letters

Example:

> In J.K. Rowling's *Harry Potter and the Chamber of Secrets*, Tom Marvolo Riddle refashioned his name to read "I am Lord Voldemort."

analects

(AN uh lekts)

a collection of passages or sayings from an author; from "things gathered up" (Greek)

Example:

> *The Analects of Confucius*

analogue

(ANN uh log)

a story whose essential plot or theme is similar in stories from several other cultures

Example:

> A notable example is The Great Flood, which is present in both the Old Testament of the Holy Bible and the *Epic of Gilgamesh*.

---

ancillary character

(ann SILL ee air ee)

secondary characters in a narrative who either contrast or complement the protagonist and also offer additional insight into the narrative's plot or theme

[*see also* chorus, characterization, foil, raisonneur]

---

anecdote

(ANN ek dote)

a short, humorous story

---

antagonist

(an TAG oh nist)

the main opposing character to the protagonist; from "opponent, rival" (Greek)

Examples:

> Teiresias is the antagonist to Oedipus in Sophocles's *Oedipus the King*.
>
> Claudius is the antagonist to Hamlet in Shakespeare's *The Tragedy of Hamlet*.
>
> Voldemort is the antagonist to Harry Potter in *Harry Potter and the Order of the Phoenix*.

[*see also* characterization, villain]

---

anticlimax

(AN tee KLAHY maks)

a sudden and unexpected culmination of events that is a disappointment in relation to the previous intensity in a narrative

also referred to as **bathos**

[*see also* plot]

anti-hero	a central character (often the protagonist) who does not exhibit the admirable qualities of the traditional hero

Examples:

Satan (*Paradise Lost*, John Milton)

Randle McMurphy (*One Flew over the Cuckoo's Nest*, Ken Kesey)

aphorism (AFF or izm)	a short, memorable statement presenting an observation, universal truth, or a principled precept to live by; a **maxim**

aphorisms are unlike proverbs in that aphorisms originate from a known author

also referred to as an **apothegm** (APP uh them), **gnomic verse** (NOH mik *or* NOM ik), or **sententia** (sin TEN shee uh *or* sin TEN shuh)

Examples:

"To thine own self be true" (*Hamlet*, I.iii, Shakespeare)

"'Tis better to have loved and lost / Than never to have loved at all" (*In Memoriam*, Alfred, Lord Tennyson)

"Fish and visitors smell in three days." (Benjamin Franklin)

"In charity there is no excess." (Francis Bacon)

apotheosis (ah PAH thee oh sis)	the elevation of a character to divine status

also referred to as **deification** (dee if uh KAY shun)

Example:

After having fought the Balrog, the character Gandalf in J.R.R. Tolkien's *The Lord of the Rings*: *The Two Towers* dies but then emerges from death as a more powerful wizard.

archaism (arr KAY izm)	a word or phrase that is no longer used in modern, common speech

Examples:

"quoth," "thine," "begat"

argot (arr GO)	slang used by social outcasts [*see also* back slang, rhyming slang]

archetype

(ARK uh tahyp)

the foundation of all characters, plots, and symbols in literature; that is, a standard character type or plot formula that recurs in literature, even across cultures; from "original form" (Greek)

the prominent psychologist Carl Jung believed that archetypes are inherent within all of mankind and interwoven throughout man's efforts in art and literature; Jung called this concept the **collective unconscious**

Example:

"the old and wise adviser"

Gandalf, *The Fellowship of the Ring* (J.R.R. Tolkien)

Dumbledore, *Harry Potter and the Sorcerer's Stone* (J.K. Rowling)

Obi-Wan Kenobi, *Star Wars: A New Hope* (1977)

[*see also* leitmotif, motif]

atmosphere

the mood or dominant feeling in a literary work

aubade

(oh BAHD)

a song about the beauty of morning or a common theme in literature that features lovers leaving one another at dawn; from "dawn song" (French)

also referred to as **alba** (AHL buh)

audience

the intended recipient(s) of a rhetorical, dramatic, narrative, or other literary presentation

back slang

a slang that is created by simply reversing words and saying them backward; popularized during the Victorian Age and first mentioned in Henry Mayhew's 1851 book *London Labour and the London Poor*

Example:

"Let's go to the beach" would be "Stel og ot eht hcaeb"

[*see also* argot, rhyming slang]

bard	a storyteller or official poet in ancient Celtic society
	the term is now synonymous with **poet**, particularly the English playwright William Shakespeare
	[*see also* gleeman]

bovarism (BOH vuh rizm)	a term to describe a daydreamer's tendency to fancy himself or herself as the hero/heroine in an adventure
	attributed to Emma Bovary, the protagonist of *Madame Bovary* (Gustave Flaubert)

Bushism (BUSH izm)	a pejorative term applied to misstatements (often malapropisms and barbarisms) by George W. Bush, the 43rd president of the United States

Examples:

> "They misunderestimated the compassion of our country. I think they misunderestimated the will and determination of the commander in chief, too." (Sept. 26, 2001)
>
> "There's no doubt in my mind, not one doubt in my mind, that we will fail." (Oct. 4, 2001)
>
> "Our enemies are innovative and resourceful, and so are we. They never stop thinking about new ways to harm our country and our people, and neither do we." (August 5, 2004)
>
> "Too many good docs are getting out of business. Too many OB/GYNs aren't able to practice their love with women all across this country." (September 6, 2004)

Byronic hero (bahy RON ik)	a proud, passionate and socially defiant rebel who harbors remorse over some past moral transgression

Examples:

> Edward Rochester (*Jane Eyre*, Charlotte Bronte)
> Heathcliff (*Wuthering Heights*, Emily Bronte)
> Rhett Butler (*Gone with the Wind*, Margaret Mitchell)

cameo	the brief appearance of a well-known character (or actor) in a work for which he or she is not the principal character

canto

one of several principal segments in a long narrative poem; a chapter or division in an epic

caricature

a literary or artistic exaggeration accomplished by distorting particular aspects of someone or something

Example:

Shakespeare exemplified anti-Semitism in his day by presenting a distorted view of Jews through his character Shylock, a Jew:

> He hates our sacred nation, and he rails,
> Even there where merchants most do congregate,
> On me, my bargains and my well-won thrift,
> Which he calls interest.
> (*The Merchant of Venice*, I.iii, Shakespeare)

carpe diem

(KAR pay DEE um)

a prominent motif, especially in the works of the Cavalier Poets, that asserts the transience of life and the necessity to enjoy life while one can; from "seize the day" (Greek)

Example:

> Gather ye rosebuds while ye may,
> Old time is still a-flying:
> And this same flower that smiles today
> Tomorrow will be dying
> ("To the Virgins, To Make Much of Time," Robert Herrick)

cataplexis

(kat uh PLEEKS sis)

prophecy or threat of retribution

Example:

> Yet know, my master, God omnipotent,
> Is mustering in his clouds on our behalf
> Armies of pestilence; and they shall strike
> Your children yet unborn and unbegot,
> That lift your vassal hands against my head
> And threat the glory of my precious crown.
> (*Richard II*, III.iii, Shakespeare)

censorship

the selective revision or removal of potentially objectionable words, passages, or entire texts

also referred to as **bowdlerization** or **expurgation**

characterization	the presentation and subsequent development of a **character**, a figure who plays a part in a narrative

direct characterization - when an author reveals a character's personality through direct, explicit statements

Example:

> "Scarlett O'Hara was not beautiful, but men seldom realized it when caught by her charm, as the Tarleton twins were." (*Gone with the Wind*, Margaret Mitchell)

indirect characterization - when an author reveals a character's personality through the character's actions, words, and interaction with others

Example:

> "And I have my own daughters to consider. I can't keep other people's children as well."
>
> The stranger hesitated and then said in a voice which he strove to make casual but which trembled slightly.
>
> "Suppose I were to take her off your hands?"
>
> "What—Cosette?"
>
> "Yes."
>
> "Why, monsieur, my dear monsieur, take her! Take her away!"
>
> (*Les Misérables*, Victor Hugo)

dynamic character - a character who changes within a story as a result of the events in the plot and the actions of other characters; these changes include, but are not limited to, emotional maturation, introspective reflection, or even a regression to baseness or evil

Examples:

> Edward Rochester in *Jane Eyre* (Charlotte Bronte)
> John the Savage in *Brave New World* (Aldous Huxley)
> Anakin Skywalker in *Star Wars: Revenge of the Sith* (2005)

static character - a character who does not change within the course of a narrative

Examples:

> St. John Rivers (*Jane Eyre*, Charlotte Bronte)
> Sodapop (*The Outsiders*, S.E. Hinton)

characterization (cont.)

flat character - a character who only has one or two personality traits and is, thus, one-dimensional in nature

Examples:

> Horatio (*Hamlet*, Shakespeare)
> Ron Weasley (*Harry Potter and the Sorcerer's Stone,* J.K. Rowling)

round character - complex, multidimensional characters; characters who have many different traits, some of which may even be in conflict

Examples:

> Jane Eyre (*Jane Eyre*, Charlotte Bronte)
> Harry Potter (*Harry Potter and the Sorcerer's Stone*, J.K. Rowling)
> Hamlet (*Hamlet*, Shakespeare)

stock character - a common, easily recognized character type that exhibits stereotyped or archetypal traits

Examples:

> The Sidekick (Samwise Gamgee, *The Lord of the Rings*, J.R.R. Tolkien)
> The Damsel in Distress (Ginny Weasley, *Harry Potter and the Chamber of Secrets*, J.K. Rowling)
> The Wise Adviser (Gandalf, The Lord of the Rings, J.R.R. Tolkien)

type character - a stereotyped trait or class

Examples:

> The Braggart; The Witty Character, The Brainy Character, etc.

[*see also* ancillary character, antagonist, anti-hero, Byronic hero, cameo, doppelgänger , epic hero, ficelle, foil, grotesque character , ingénue, hero/heroine, protagonist, raisonneur]

Chekhov's gun	refers to a prop , character, or plot element introduced early in a narrative but whose importance is not revealed until later in the story; coined by author Anton Chekhov; also referred to as **repetitive designation**

Examples:

> The pistol in *Uncle Vanya* (Anton Chekhov)
>
> The Ring of Power in *The Lord of the Rings* trilogy (J.R.R. Tolkien)
>
> Fortinbras in *Hamlet* (Shakespeare)

chreia (KRAY uh)	referring to a person through an anecdote in order to inspire or teach; from "useful" (Greek)

Example:

> "How well I remember the aged poet Sophocles, when in answer to the question, 'How does lovemaking suit with old age, Sophocles, —are you still the man you were?' 'Peace, he replied; most gladly have I escaped the thing of which you speak; I feel as if I had escaped from a mad and furious master.' His words have often occurred to my mind since, and they seem as good to me now as at the time when he uttered them. For certainly old age has a great sense of calm and freedom; when the passions relax their hold, then, as Sophocles says, 'We are freed from the grasp not of one mad master only, but of many.'" (*The Republic*, Plato)

clausula (KLAW zhuh luh)	the rhythmic closing of a prose sentence, often with a cadence similar to that employed by the Latin orator Cicero

colloquial (kuh LOKE kwee ill)	informal, conversational language; the noun form is **colloquialism** (kuh LOKE kwee ill izm) also referred to as **vernacular** and is described often as **demotic** (language of the common people)

Examples:

> "Hey, y'all, how y'all doin'?"
>
> "Wazzup?"

[*see also* local color, slang]

comic relief

a humorous character or situation inserted into a tragedy or other somber work

Example:

the porter scene in Shakespeare's *Macbeth* (II.iii)

complication

plot events that occur in the rising action and intensify the climax

Example:

In Shakespeare's *Hamlet*, Laertes's and Hamlet's swords are switched. In addition, Gertrude, Hamlet's mother, drinks from a poisoned cup, which was intended for Hamlet.

concrete diction

consists of specific words that describe physical qualities or manifestations; concrete diction creates a mental picture and is something the observer (reader) can touch, smell, see, hear, or taste

abstract diction, on the other hand, creates a vague, often ambiguous, image

Example:

"Susan and Kurt drank double lattes at Starbucks."

[The words *drank*, *lattes*, and *Starbucks* are all concrete because they are things an observer can see or experience in a tangible way.]

concrete universal

the articulation of a general idea with concrete images

examples include **allegories** and **parables**

connotation

(kahn oh TAY shun)

the underlying meaning of a word or phrase; may include implicit suggestions or associations as well as tone

Examples:

"My friend is strong-willed."

"My friend is stubborn."

Strong-willed and *stubborn* both mean the same thing in a literal sense. However, *strong-willed* connotes admiration whereas *stubborn* suggests negativity.

also:

Although the word *wall* literally means a physical structure, it could also suggest a non-physical obstacle or hindrance.

[*see also* context, denotation]

---

context

the information before or after a text that helps clarify the underlying meaning of the text itself

[*see also* connotation]

---

controlling image

a dominant image an author or poet uses to develop the meaning of a work

Example:

Shakespeare uses the controlling image of the North Star in "Sonnet 116":

O no! it is an ever-fixed mark

That looks on tempests and is never shaken;

It is the star to every wandering bark,

Whose worth's unknown, although his height be taken.

---

convention

a literary form or device that is standard and expected within a specific genre or style

also referred to as a **literary convention**

[*see also* dramatic convention, epic convention]

courtly love	a code of behavior popularized in the Middle Ages in which women were idealized and revered in a platonic, non-sexual way
	this concept was popularized by poet performers in the south of France known as **troubadours** (TROO buh doorz)
counter-turn	a surprising plot or character development in a story
	also referred to as a **coup de théâtre** or **plot twist**
danse macabre (DAHNS muh KAH bruh)	a visual representation of the figure of death leading a processional death march; from "dance of death" (French)
deixis (DAHYK sis)	words that depend on a particular context to have true meaning **Examples:** I/you; here/there; now/then [The pronouns *I* and *you* can refer to the same person but in different contexts, just as the adverbs *here* and *there* can refer to the same place, but their respective meanings change by context.]
denotation (dee no TAY shun)	a word's dictionary definition rather than any implied meaning [*see also* connotation, context]
details	specific facts that are included or omitted as part of a writer's style **Example with details**: "The old desk was covered with past due forms, useless pens, and dried out Liquid Paper bottles." **Example without details**: "The desk was cluttered."
deus ex machina (DAY ihs eks MAHK in uh)	to describe a contrived (disingenuously coincidental) event in a literary work or film; from "God from the machine" (Greek)

device

a technique or figure of speech used to achieve a specific literary effect

dialect

a distinct, nonstandard variety of a language particular to a geographic region or social group

Example:

"'Don't you give me none o' your lip,' says he. 'You've put on considerable many frills since I been away. I'll take you down a peg before I get done with you...Who told you you might meddle with such hifalut'n foolishness, hey? -- who told you you could?'" (*The Adventures of Huckleberry Finn*, Mark Twain)

diction

an author's word choice; can be categorized in three forms:

- **low diction** (slang, vernacular)
- **middle diction** (conversational)
- **elevated (high) diction** (formal)

Examples of low, middle, and elevated diction:

Low:

"Man, you some kind of crazy thinking your hoopty is going to get you some girls."

Middle:

"I don't think your car is going to help you attract women."

Elevated:

"It is unforeseeable that your automobile will enamor the opposite sex."

Examples of weak diction and strong diction:

Weak diction:

"My friends like to go out on the weekend."

Strong diction:

"On the weekend, my friends Jason and Sara like to eat at Chili's and then go to Tinseltown to see an action movie."

[*see also* abstract diction, concrete diction, connotation, denotation, dialect, jargon, slang]

diegetic (dahy eh JEE tik)	the events being narrated in a story as distinct from the telling of the narrative the narration, which includes elements outside the principal elements of the story, is known as (the **extradiegetic** (EKS truh dahy uh JEE tik) level) a story within a story is the **hypodiogetic** (HYE poh dahy uh JEE tik) level
discourse	a discussion or lengthy work on a sustained topic
discovery	when a major character is given previously unknown information or insight; usually appears in the climax or dénouement [*see also* anagnorisis]
donnée (dah NAY)	a set of principles, assumptions, or scenario upon which a literary work is based; from "something given" (French)

doppelgänger
 	
(DOP uhl gang er)
	a look-alike or a non-related twin, whose presence usually forebodes ill; in folklore, the spirit double of a living person
	
	Examples of works incorporating a doppelgänger:
	    "William Wilson" (Edgar Allan Poe)
	    "Der Doppelgänger" (Heinrich Heine)
	    The Dark Half (Stephen King)

eggcorn

the replacement of a word or phrase with a similar sounding word or phrase that sounds like a plausible replacement, but is still incorrect

coined by linguist Geoffrey Pullum

Examples (correct usage is the latter of each pair):

"old-timer's disease" for "Alzheimer's disease"
"baited breath" for "bated breath"
"hone in" for "horne in"
"agging it on" for "egging it on"

[*see also* malapropism, mondegreen]

emblem

an image or object that has a fixed representational meaning

[*see also* icon, symbol]

enigma

(eh NIG muh)

a puzzle or **riddle**; something that has a hidden meaning or is hard to interpret; ambiguous

Example:

"What is it that walks on four feet and two feet and three feet and has only one voice, and when it walks on most feet it is the weakest?" (the Sphinx's riddle to Oedipus in Sophocles's *Oedipus the King*)

epic hero

the protagonist in a epic who possesses many, if not all, of the following qualities:

- is the embodiment of a nation or people
- has unusual circumstances surrounding his birth or childhood
- possesses superior strength and is extraordinarily brave
- gives an inspirational speech to followers
- is often aided by deities or other supernatural creatures
- undergoes a journey, which involves temptations or other internal conflicts
- often descends into the underworld as part of a journey of self-awareness or quest
- faces final task alone

Examples:

Beowulf (*Beowulf*), Odysseus (*The Odyssey*), Achilles (*The Iliad*)

epigram

(EPP ih gram)

a brief, witty statement in verse form, often as an inscription

Example:

"We think our fathers fools, so wise we grow, / Our wise sons, no doubt, will think us so." (Alexander Pope)

[*see also* jeu d'esprit]

epiphany

(ih PIF uh nee)

a character's sudden understanding of the significance of an object or situation; from "manifestation" or "showing-forth" (Greek)

Example:

In Shakespeare's *Hamlet* (II.ii), after having seen an outburst of emotion from an actor performing a piece on Hecuba and Priam, Hamlet realizes that he must show greater passion and act on his conscience.

[*see also* anagnorisis]

episode

a moment or situation that is independent, but may be related, to other moments or situations in a literary work; from "parenthetic narrative" (Greek)

a work that is composed in such a way is referred to as **episodic** (epp ih SAHD ik)

eponymous work

(uh PON uh miss)

a work that is named for the protagonist, hero, or the author (artist); from "giving the name to" (Greek)

the noun form is **eponym**

Examples of novels named for their protagonists:

Silas Marner (George Eliot)

David Copperfield (Charles Dickens)

Scarlett (Alexandra Ripley)

Farberism

(FAR burr izm)

a term coined to describe idiom blends and twisted clichés popularized by noted computer science professor David Farber (Carnegie Mellon University)

Examples:

"We have a difference of agreement."

"Let's not cook the goose until it's hatched."

"Nostalgia just isn't what it used to be."

"From here on up, it's downhill all the way."

[*see also* Yogiism]

ficelle

(FISS ull)

a term Henry James coined to describe a character whose role as an insider gives the reader important information apart from the narrator

[*see also* characterization]

flashback

a literary device in which the author presents events from an earlier time (usually having occurred before the setting of the current narrative); flashbacks are usually presented as dreams or memories

also referred to as **analepsis** (ann uh LEP sis)

Example:

The majority of the plot of J.K. Rowling's *Harry Potter and the Half-Blood Prince* is written as a flashback to when Voldemort was a young Tom Riddle and presented by Dumbledore through the use of a pensieve.

---

focalization

a story's point of view

events recounted by an omniscient narrator are **non-focalized**

events recounted by a single character are **internally focalized**

---

foil

an ancillary character who is a direct opposite to the protagonist and whose purpose is to magnify the protagonist's traits

Examples:

St. John Rivers is a foil for Rochester in *Jane Eyre* (Charlotte Bronte).

Laertes and Fortinbras are foils for Hamlet in *Hamlet* (Shakespeare).

Banquo is a foil for Macbeth in *Macbeth* (Shakespeare).

[*see also* characterization]

---

foreshadowing

device a writer uses to allude to a future event in a story

Example:

Shirley Jackson uses foreshadowing near the beginning of her short story "The Lottery":

"Bobby Martin had already stuffed his pockets full of stones, and the other boys soon followed his example, selecting the smoothest and roundest stones. . . . "

[This sentence foreshadows the stoning scene at the end of the story.]

[*see also* prolepsis]

form	the general structure of a literary work, especially as it relates to its genre
	elements of form include syntactical and organizational elements as well as literary devices
fustian	overly ornate, pretentious language
	also referred to as **euphuism** (YOO fyoo izm) (not to be confused with *euphemism*)
frame story	a narrative that serves as the introduction of another narrative; a story embedded within another story
	also referred to as a **frame narrative**
	the stories within a frame story are said to be **embedded stories**
	Examples:
	The Canterbury Tales (Chaucer)
	The Scarlet Letter (Nathaniel Hawthorne)
gallows humor	macabre humor, often with the intention to desensitize the horrific nature of disease, trauma, or death
	Examples:
	"Ask for me to-morrow, and you shall find me a grave man." (*Romeo and Juliet*, III.iii, Shakespeare)
gasconade (gas kuh NADE)	a character's excessive bragging or boasting
	[*see also* alazon (within the entry for eiron)]
ghost word	a neologism that results from a typographical error or mondegreen
	also referred to as a **phantom word**
	Examples:
	"willy-nilly" (a mondegreen from "will he, nill he?")
	"pwn" (a typographical error of "own," a term that means to dominate another in a video game)

ghostwriter	a person who is employed to write a finished manuscript for another person, who is the presumed author
gleeman	a wandering Medieval singer or minstrel [*see also* bard]
Great Chain of Being, the	a prominent concept in Medieval and Renaissance literature that orders everything in the universe in an interdependent hierarchy this chain, which contains several divisions and subdivisions, is essentially ordered in the following way (from lowest (at the bottom) to highest (at the top)):

God

angels

man

woman

animals

vegetation

greater elements (gold and silver)

rocks and minerals

griot (GREE ott *or* GREE oh)	a West-African storyteller and performer [*see also* bard, scop]
grotesque character	a character that inspires both pity and disgust **Examples:** Quasimodo (*The Hunchback of Notre Dame*, Victor Hugo) Erik (The Phantom) (*The Phantom of the Opera*, Gaston Leroux)
hack	a negative term applied to writers who produce inferior or disreputable works; a hack writer is also often referred to as a **Grub Street** writer

hero/heroine	a chief character of a work (usually, but not always, the protagonist) who expresses admirable qualities such as courage, wisdom, or nobility
	
	Examples:
	    Jane Eyre (*Jane Eyre*, Charlotte Bronte)
	    Harry Potter (*Harry Potter* series, J.K. Rowling)
	    Luke Skywalker (*Star Wars, Episodes 4-6, 1977-1983*)
	
	[*see also* anti-hero]

heteroglossia (HET ih roh GLOSS ee uh)	a term coined by Russian literary critic Mikhail Bakhtin to describe the competing variations of language and voice among the author, narrator, and characters

Homeric epithet	compound adjectives applied to a noun; used frequently by Homer
	
	Examples:
	    "**rosy-fingered** dawn" (*The Odyssey*, Homer)
	    "**swift-footed** Achilles" (*The Iliad*, Homer)

humors, the	a common element in Medieval and Renaissance literature that defined a character's dominant personality traits; based on the belief that humans were composed of four elements (humors) and usually had one or two that dominated the others:
	
	    • **blood** (affable yet prone to self-indulgence)
	    • **phlegm** (calm and resistant to change)
	    • **black bile** (irritable and depressed)
	    • **yellow bile** (hot-tempered and passionate)
	
	also spelled **humours**

hypostatization (hahy POSS tuh tih ZAY shun)	a type of personification in which an abstraction is given human qualities **Example:** "Love does not wait—it seeks."

icon

a widely recognized symbol or representative object

contrast with **iconoclast**, which is someone or something that actively attacks the representative nature of an icon or established traditions and institutions

[*see also* defamiliarization]

idée fixe

(ee day FEEKS)

a recurrent theme or motif; from "fixed idea" (French)

[*see also* archetype, leitmotif]

idiolect

(ID ee oh lekt)

a style of language particular to an individual

[*see also* dialect, vernacular]

imagery

words or expressions that stimulate one or more of the senses: sight (visual), taste (gustatory), touch (tactile), hearing (auditory), and smell (olfactory)

in medias res

(in MAY dee us RACE)

the technique of beginning a narrative in the middle of the action; from "in the middle of things" (Latin)

crucial events preceding the action are usually revealed through flashbacks

in medias res is an epic convention

Example:

Book I of John Milton's *Paradise Lost* opens in Hell, into which Satan and other fallen angels have been thrown as a result of an unsuccessful attempt to overthrow God in Heaven. The actual civil war is not described until Book VI.

incluing

(in KLOO ing)

the gradual revelation of a fantastical world as a form of plot exposition

Examples:

> In J.K. Rowling's *Harry Potter* series, Hermione Granger and Albus Dumbledore gradually reveal aspects of the witching world simultaneously to Harry Potter and to the readers.
>
> The Controller reveals aspects of the "brave new world" to John the Savage in Aldous Huxley's *Brave New World*.

[*see also* topothesia]

ingénue

(AHN zhuh noo)

a naïve young female protagonist

Examples:

> Snow White ("Snow White," the Brothers Grimm)
>
> Giselle (*Enchanted*, 2007)

inscape/instress

terms used by the poet Gerard Manley Hopkins to describe the essential unique, dynamic nature of an object (the inscape) and the divine energy that reveals the true nature of the object (the instress)

invocation

(inn voh KAY shun)

a poet's appeal made to a deity or a muse for insight or inspiration; particularly common in epics

Example:

> Sing heavenly Muse, that on the secret top
> Of Oreb, or of Sinai, didst inspire
> That shepherd, who first taught the chosen seed,
> In the beginning how the heavens and earth
> Rose out of chaos
> (*Paradise Lost*, Book I, John Milton)

jargon

(JAR gun)

words and phrases particular to a given profession or group; often meant to indicate language that is intended to exclude by way of acronyms and **specialized vocabulary**

Examples:

> **Educational/Research jargon:** "The longitudinal study indicated a regression to the mean."
>
> **Legal jargon:** "The court refused to issue a writ of certiorari for that case."

jeremiad

(jare uh MAHY edd)

a lengthy lamentation or prophecy of doom

jeu d'esprit

(ZHEH des PREE)

a clever, yet light-hearted, witty remark; from "a game of the spirit" (French)

also referred to as a **bon mot** (bohn MOH)

Examples:

"Young people, nowadays, imagine that money is everything, and when they grow older they know it." (Oscar Wilde)

"Women are meant to be loved, not to be understood." (Oscar Wilde)

"I can resist everything except temptation." (Oscar Wilde)

"Go to Heaven for the climate, Hell for the company. " (Mark Twain)

[*see also* epigram]

jongleur

(JONG glurr)

a traveling entertainer in medieval Europe

jumped the shark

a term that refers to any piece of serial entertainment that has outlived its popularity

derives from an episode of the television show *Happy Days*, in which a popular character, the Fonz, wearing water-skis and his trademark black leather jacket, literally jumps over a shark; many viewers and critics felt that this episode was the moment in which the popular show had lost its appeal

King's English, the

formal English spoken and written properly; contrast with colloquialisms, slang, and vernacular

language

how one communicates to others; specifically, the diction, details, syntax, and imagery used to convey a writer's style

Latinate

(LAT in ATE)

used to denote language that imitates the style of the Latin language, such as using words with Latin (rather than Old English) origins or inverting the syntax of a line or sentence

Example:

And who knows,
Let this be good, whether our angry Foe
Can give it, or will ever? How he can
Is doubtful; that he never will is sure.
(*Paradise Lost*, Book II, John Milton)

legendarium

(lej in DARE ee um)

literally, a collection of legends; usually, however, this term specifically refers to the legends of Middle-Earth created by author J.R.R. Tolkien

leitmotif

(LAHYT moh teef)

the dominant recurring themes or patterns of a work; from "leading motive" (German)

[*see also* archetype, idée fixe, motif]

lingo

an informal term that refers to a foreign language or dialect; from "tongue" (Latin)

lingua franca

(LING gwah FRANG kah)

a language that serves as an intermediary between two other languages; from "Frankish tongue" (Italian)

Examples:

For a person who speaks English and French only and a person who speaks Japanese and French only, French would be the lingua franca.

The English language is the lingua franca of all international aviation communications.

local color	a writer's use of detail that captures the customs, manners, speech, folklore, and other qualities of a particular region or community

Example:

> Mark Twain is well known as a local colorist, particularly in his novel *The Adventures of Tom Sawyer*:
>
> > "Tom, it was middling warm in school, warn't it?"
> >
> > "Yes'm."
> >
> > "Powerful warm, warn't it?"
> >
> > "Yes'm."
> >
> > "Didn't you want to go in a-swimming, Tom?"
> >
> > A bit of a scare shot through Tom--a touch of uncomfortable suspicion. He searched Aunt Polly's face, but it told him nothing.

[*see also* dialect, regional novel, vernacular]

logrolling	the practice of trading favorable book reviews among authors

longueur (LAWN gurr)	a long passage that drags on unnecessarily

machiavellian (mack ee uh VELL ee un)	refers to a character who is unscrupulous, deceitful, and manipulative derived from Niccolo Machiavelli's work *The Prince*

Examples of machiavellian characters:

> Iago (*Othello*, Shakespeare)
>
> Richard III (*Richard III*, Shakespeare)
>
> Machevil (*The Jew of Malta*, Christopher Marlowe)

macrocosm	the world as a whole; society in general [*see also* microcosm]

malapropism

(MAL uh prop izm)

malapropisms are a type of word confusion in which a word is substituted with a similar word resulting in a comic effect (whether unintentional or not)

a type of **acyrologia** (ak ir oh LOH jee ah), which is a mistaken use of similar sounding words

Examples:

> "O villain! thou wilt be condemned into everlasting **redemption** [perdition] for this." (*Much Ado about Nothing*, IV.ii, Shakespeare)

> "We cannot let terrorists and rogue nations hold this nation **hostile** [hostage] or hold our allies **hostile** [hostage]." (President George W. Bush, 2000)

[*see also* Bushism, eggcorn, mondegreen, Yogiism]

media

(MEE dee uh)

a general term usually reserved for periodicals and televised programs devoted to reporting the news

also refers to any collection of audiovisual materials

a single channel of communication is called a **medium**

The following are terms attributed to specific embodiments of the media:

> the **Fourth Estate** – the press in general
> the **Fourth Branch** of government – the American press
> **Fleet Street** – the British press

microcosm

a smaller representation of a larger world

Examples:

> In William Golding's novel *The Lord of the Flies*, the island on which children take on the negative characteristics of adults is a microcosm of society at large.

> In Shirley Jackson's short story "The Lottery," the village is a microcosm representing backward ideas in the world at large.

[*see also* macrocosm, simulacrum]

mimesis

(muh MEE sis)

representation of the real world in art and literature; from "an imitation" (Greek)

minimalism	a literary style that reduces the elements of a text to its bare minimum, usually manifested by sparse vocabulary and economy of form

mise-en-abyme (meez en ah BEEM)	a frame story that contains a duplication of itself in the narrative; a looping of the story with no seeming end; from "into the abyss" (French)

Examples:

> *The Counterfeiters* (André Gide)
>
> "The Garden of Forking Paths" (Jorge Luis Borges)

mock heroic	the use of lofty style, including epic similes and other epic devices, that elevates something that is actually base or trivial; often found in parodies or satires

Examples:

> For, that sad moment, when the Sylphs withdrew,
> And Ariel weeping from Belinda flew,
> Umbriel, a dusky, melancholy Sprite,
> As ever sully'd the fair Face of Light,
> Down to the Central Earth, his proper Scene,
> Repair'd to search the gloomy Cave of Spleen.
> (*The Rape of the Lock*, Alexander Pope)

[*see also* mock epic]

mondegreen

(MAHN duh green)

a mistaken word or phrase resulting from a mishearing of a song or something said

coined by Sylvia Wright in 1954 to describe a misinterpreted line of the ballad "The Bonnie Earl O'Murray"

mondegreens are a type of word confusion called **acyrologia** (ak ir oh LOH jee ah)

Examples:

> Wright mistook the last line of the ballad "The Bonnie Earl O'Murray" as "And Lady Mondegreen," which was actually "And laid him on the green."

> Another example offered by Wright is "Surely Good Mrs. Murphy shall follow me all the days of my life" for "Surely goodness and mercy shall follow me all the days of my life" from Psalms 23.

[*see also* eggcorn, homophone, malapropism, mosaic rhyme]

mood

the atmosphere felt in a work either by the characters or by the reader

Example:

> The events of Charlotte Bronte's *Jane Eyre* and Emily Bronte's *Wuthering Heights* are often set in a gloomy atmosphere, creating a suspenseful mood.

moral

a literary work's overall didactic message (i.e., what is supposed to be learned from the work)

Example:

> The moral of Aesop's "Tortoise and the Hare" is to be determined rather than speedy.

[*see also* didactic literature]

motif

(moh TEEF)

a recurring theme in a literary work or in literature in general

[see also archetype, idée fixe, leitmotif]

motivation

a mixture of situation and personality that compels a character to behave the way he or she does

also referred to as **character motive**

Examples:

Anakin Skywalker's motivation to turn to the dark side in *Star Wars: Revenge of the Sith* (2005) begins with his fear of losing his wife, Padme.

Jane Eyre's (*Jane Eyre,* Charlotte Bronte) motivation to leave Edward Rochester is her anguish after Edward's brother-in-law claims that Edward was already married.

muse

a poet or writer's source of inspiration; often referred to in epic poetry

derives from Greek mythology in which the nine Muses, who were daughters of Zeus and Mnemosyne (goddess of memory), directed various aspects of the arts

mythopoeic

(mith oh PEE ik)

inclined to create and sustain myths that serve as a basis for explaining the origin and the workings of the world and one's society

naïve narrator

a narrator who is too innocent and unschooled in the ways of the world to understand situations or other characters fully and, thus, presents a skewed (and sometimes unreliable) account of events

Example:

Candide (*Candide*, Voltaire)

[*see also* narrator, point of view]

narratology

the study and analysis of narrator types and narrative structures

narrator	the speaker through whom the author presents a story; the storyteller

two notable variations are the **reliable narrator**, who tells the events in the story and describes the characters in an objective way, and the **unreliable narrator**, who may be misleading, biased, or otherwise faulty in the accounting of the story

Examples:

> *The Underground Man* is Fyodor Dostoevsky's narrator of the novel of the same name. He is who recounts the events of the story.

> Examples of unreliable narrators can be found in Fyodor Dostoevsky's *The Underground Man*, William Faulkner's *The Sound and the Fury*, and Daniel Keyes's *Flowers for Algernon*.

[*see also* naïve narrator, point of view]

neologism (nee OLL uh jizm)	a recently coined word that has gained mainstream use; can be the result of the combining of words (portmanteau)

Examples:

> "blog" (web log)

> "red states and blue states" (in a political sense, states and commonwealths that lean Republican and Democrat, respectively)

[*see also* ghost word]

Nine Worthies, the	notable historical figures alluded to in medieval literature and identified by William Caxton in the preface to *Le Morte D'Arthur*: Alexander, Hector, Julius Caesar (Pagan); David, Joshua, Judas Maccabeus (Jewish); Arthur, Charlemagne, Godfrey of Bouillon (Christian)

Noble Savage, the	a character or ideal that represents simplicity and primitive goodness, particularly in contrast to rampant industrialization and materialism

Examples of the noble savage:

Queequeg (*Moby Dick*, Herman Melville)
Friday (*Robinson Crusoe*, Daniel Defoe)
Chief Bromden (*One Flew over the Cuckoo's Nest*, Ken Kesey)
John the Savage (*Brave New World*, Aldous Huxley)

nonce word	a word created for a specific purpose and not meant for mainstream use; however, some nonce words have become neologisms, which are newly coined words adopted into mainstream language

Examples of nonce words:

"mileconsuming" (*Light in August*, William Faulkner)
"supercalifragilisticexpialidocious" (1964 musical *Mary Poppins*)

Examples of nonce words that have become neologisms:

"jabberwocky" ("Jabberwocky," Lewis Carroll)
"quark" (*Ulysses*, James Joyce)

obiter dicta (OH bih turr DIK tah)	various comments and sayings of a person collected in conversation; from "things said by the way" (Latin) [*see also* analects]

oeuvre (UHR vruh)	the complete works of a writer or an artist; from "work" (French) also referred to as a **corpus**; from "a body," Latin

onomatomania (on uh maht uh MAY nee uh)	a compulsion to repeat certain words or names or simply an obsession with those words or names; from "name crazy" (Greek) **Example:** CHARLIE: You know how to dance, Ray? RAYMOND: No. CHARLIE: I'll have to teach you sometime. RAYMOND: **Definitely** have to dance on my date. Have to learn how to dance. **Definitely**. Now. CHARLIE: Ray, you're not gonna have to dance, but I will teach you sometime. RAYMOND: **Definitely** have to dance with Iris. (*Rain Man*, 1988)
order of ideas	a method of organization in writing; how a work is developed **cause-effect**—organization that details the result of an action or event **chronological order**—organization of events in a narrative as they happened (such as relating a childhood memory) **compare-contrast**—organization that features similarities and differences of two or more subjects **order of importance**—organization of subjects prioritized by the author **problem/solution order**—organization that defines a problem and then enumerates the steps to solving the problem **spatial/geographic order**—organization of subjects by placement (such as a description of an outdoor scene) **taxonomic order**—the ordering of items by groups and sub-groups (such as a description of a type of animal)
organic form	refers to works that are not bound by established conventions but rather develop as the theme or subject unfolds, thereby creating a unique pattern of literature or art

paraphrase (PAIR uh frayz)	to restate a text in other words [*see also* summary]
pastiche (pass TEESH)	the imitation of words, phrases, or complete passages used in another work, usually with the intention of flattery; from "paste" (Italian) contrast pastiche with parody, which is intended to ridicule or mock the original work
pastoral imagery (PASS tore ull)	images of a rural setting praising a rustic way of life; also referred to as **bucolic imagery**
pathetic fallacy (puh THET ik FAL uh see)	a type of personification in which elements of nature or animals display humanlike emotions or responses **Example:** "Lo, the most excellent sun so calm and haughty" ("When Lilacs Last in the Dooryard Bloom'd," Walt Whitman)
patron	a benefactor who supports an artist either institutionally, inspirationally, or monetarily
persona (purr SOH nah)	the speaker in any first-person poem or narrative; the persona is the author's voice but may not always reflect the author's personal opinions, feelings, or perspectives on a subject; from "mask" (Latin) **Example:** Fyodor Dostoevsky's persona in *The Underground Man* is the narrator, who is capricious and often demonstrates contempt for others in society, which does not necessarily reflect Dostoevsky's personal beliefs.

personification (purr SAHN if uh kay shun)	referring to inanimate objects, abstractions, or animals as if they were human also referred to as **prosopopoeia** **Examples:** "Because I could not stop for *Death / He* kindly **stopped** for me" (Emily Dickinson) "Or **Jealousy** with rankling tooth, / That inly **gnaws** the secret heart" ("Ode on a Distant Prospect of Eton College," Thomas Gray) [*see also* anthropomorphism, hypostatization, pathetic fallacy]
phallic symbol (FAL ik SIM bull)	an image or representation in literature of the penis; suggested interpretations have included dominance and fertility **Examples:** Often, metaphorically protruding objects have been interpreted as phallic symbols: keys, towers, jets, shovels, etc. Eudora Welty's character Manley Pointer in her story "Good Country People" has a phallic name that befits his wanton, dominant personality. [*see also* yonic symbol]
phantasmagoria (fan TAZ muh gore ee uh)	a continually shifting, haphazardly presented dreamlike sequence of related images **Example:** The shadow of the dome of pleasure Floated midway on the waves ; Where was heard the mingled measure From the fountain and the caves. It was a miracle of rare device, A sunny pleasure-dome with caves of ice ! A damsel with a dulcimer In a vision once I saw : It was an Abyssinian maid, And on her dulcimer she played, Singing of Mount Abora. Could I revive within me Her symphony and song, To such a deep delight 'twould win me, ("Kubla Khan," Samuel Taylor Coleridge)

philistine (FILL ih stine)	a person who does not seem to appreciate or understand the finer aspects of literature the arts
pirated	a work that has been taken either in part or in whole with no compensation or attribution to the author
plagiarism (PLAY juh rizm)	the unauthorized use of text with no references or attribution, specifically for the purpose of taking credit for the text without acknowledging the original author's claims of authorship; from "kidnapper; thief" (Latin) [*see also* pastiche]
plausible action	an action by a character that seems reasonable based on prevailing circumstances and motivations

plot
the arrangement of related events in a prose narrative or drama; the underlying structure of a story

a **pyramidal pattern** refers to the basic plot structure of a prose narrative:

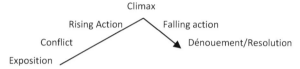

exposition—a plot element in which the characters and the setting of a story are introduced

conflict—the opposition of two forces or characters; an **internal conflict** occurs within one character (such as emotional turmoil or doubts), and an **external conflict** occurs between a character and another character, society, or a force of nature

rising action— the point of increasing intensity between opposing elements in a narrative, resulting in the climax (also referred to as the **crisis**)

climax—the part of a narrative that contains the height of action and the most intensity

falling action—the events following the major climax of a plot that lead to an end in the resolution of the plot

dénouement—(day noo MAW) the **resolution** of a plot—when all of the conflicts in a narrative are solved or untangled; from "unknotting" (French)

[*see also* anticlimax, complication, discovery, Freytag's Pyramid]

poetic justice
a literary feature by which good is rewarded and evil is punished

poetic license
the artistic freedom given to poets and authors to depart from normal standards of syntax, grammar, or pronunciation to achieve a more satisfying imaginative or metrical effect

also referred to as **artistic license** or **dramatic license**

point of view

whose thoughts and feelings the reader has access to

first person point of view—when the narrator of a story is also a character in the story

second person point of view—when the narrator of a work addresses the reader directly with the use of the personal pronoun *you* (used more frequently in works of nonfiction rather than fiction)

third person point of view—a point of view in which the narrator does not interact with the story but is, rather, an observer to the action; includes the following types:

> **omniscient point of view**—when the narrator of a story is "all knowing;" a point of view in which the narrator can recount the actions, thoughts, and feelings of any character at any time

> **limited point of view**—when the narrator of a story is outside the story and tells the story from the vantage point of only one character at a time

> **editorial omniscience**—a point of view in which the all-knowing narrator (known as an **intrusive narrator**) guides the reader to a judgment about a character or a situation

> **objective point of view**—also referred to as **dramatic point of view** or **neutral omniscience**; a point of view in which the narrator (considered a **reliable narrator**) gives only the information that can be observed without inference, allowing the reader to make an independent judgment about a character or situation

> [*see also* ficelle, focalization, naïve narrator, narrator, speaker, stream of consciousness, unreliable narrator]

portmanteau
 	
(port man TOH)
	a word created by combining two different words into one; a type of **neologism**
	
	coined by Lewis Carroll in *Through the Looking Glass*, in which he invents the word *slithy* from *lithe* and *slimy*
	
	Examples:
	    "prequel" (pre + sequel)
	    "brunch" (breakfast + lunch)
	    "smog" (smoke + fog)
	    "frenemy" (friend + enemy)

potboiler	a literary work with little or no literary merit, solely meant to produce income for the author also referred to as **kitsch** (KICH)

prolepsis
 	
(proh LEEP sis)
	a looking-forward in a story; an anticipation or prophecy of what is to come, or the labeling of something that will exist in the future to the present or past
	
	also referred to as a **flash-forward**
	
	Examples:
	    The prophecy told to Oedipus that he will sleep with his mother and kill his father. (*Oedipus the King*, Sophocles)
	    When Hamlet says to his friend, "I am dead, Horatio" (*Hamlet*, V.ii, Shakespeare)
	    "...the pre-colonial United States"
	
	[*see also* procatalepsis]

prose	written language that is not poetry (verse), drama, or song prose is either fiction or nonfiction; novels, essays, and short stories are the most common types of prose

protagonist

(proh TAG oh nist)

the principal character in a narrative

Examples:

Jane Eyre (*Jane Eyre*, Charlotte Bronte)

Harry Potter (*Harry Potter and the Sorcerer's Stone*, J.K. Rowling)

Satan (*Paradise Lost*, John Milton)

---

proverb

(PRAH vurb)

a short popular saying of unknown origin

also referred to as an **adage**

Example:

"Too many cooks spoil the broth."

[*see also* aphorism]

---

pseudonym

(SOO doh nim)

a fictitious name used by a writer; also referred to as a **pen name** or **nom de plume**

Examples:

Mark Twain (Samuel Clemens)

George Eliot (Mary Ann Evans)

A.N. Roquelure (Ann Rice)

Richard Saunders (Benjamin Franklin)

Richard Bachmann (Stephen King)

---

pseudo-statement

(SOO doh STATE mint)

a term coined by I.A. Richards to denote an emotional statement in poetry or fiction that cannot be empirically verified, yet maintains an element of truth or relevance

---

psychomachy

(sahy KAHM ih kee)

a literary theme that focuses on the battle for a person's soul and features supernatural forces representing good and evil

Examples:

prominent in the following works: *Doctor Faustus*, *Everyman*

[*see also* morality play]

---

purple patch

a negative term applied to an overly ornate or overly worded passage that does not seem to contribute to the text as a whole

Pyrrhic victory

(PIR ik)

a victory that is accompanied by enormous losses, leaving a devastating cost to the victor

also referred to as a **Cadmean victory** (kad MEE un)

Examples:

the Greeks' defeat of the Trojan army in Homer's *The Iliad*

the defeat of the Separatists during the Clone Wars (*Star Wars: Revenge of the Sith*, 2005)

"Another such victory over the Romans, and we are undone." (Pyrrhus, from Plutarch's *Life of Pyrrhus*)

raisonneur

(rez uh NURR)

an ancillary character who is involved, but often passively, in the plot and offers insight on the characters and the overriding themes of the work

Example:

Horatio (*Hamlet*, Shakespeare)

[*see also* characterization]

rebus

(REE bus)

a word or phrase represented by pictures or symbols

Example:

a picture of a bee and a leaf could represent the word *believe*

rhapsody

(RAP soh dee)

a work or part of a work that is particularly impassioned

rhetorical mode

(ruh TORE ih kull mode)

refers to the intended purpose(**mode**) of a writing (e.g., persuasive, narrative, expository)

these modes can also have more specific purposes (**author's purpose**): to entertain, to inform, or to explain

rhyming slang

a type of code used by speakers of the Cockney dialect in England

consists of rhyming a coded word in the second word of a two-word phrase; adaptations of this slang drop the second word (the rhyme)

Examples:

"Apples and pears" for "stairs"

"loaf" for "head" (originating as "loaf of bread")

"Barney Rubble" for "trouble"

BASHER: So unless we intend to do this job in Reno, we're in barney.

[everyone pauses]

BASHER: Barney Rubble.

[everyone looks confused]

BASHER: Trouble!

(*Ocean's Eleven*, 2001)

[*see also* argot, back slang]

rite of passage

a ritual or event that marks a change in a character's status; a "coming of age"

[*see also* bildungsroman]

rococo

(ruh KOH koh *or* roh kuh KOH)

an ornate, lighthearted writing style

rune

a symbol, often inscribed in stone, that represents a supernatural power

sarcasm

harsh language or a bitter denunciation presented in a mockingly positive way

Examples:

"'I'm sure you're the fastest person here! I guess we'll see in a couple of seconds,'" said the runner to his competition."

scatological

(SKAT uh lahj uh kull)

references to human excrement

Example:

Jonathan Swift's *Gulliver's Travels* employs scatological humor:

"I had been for some hours extremely pressed by the necessities of nature; which was no wonder, it being almost two days since I had last disburdened myself. I was under great difficulties between urgency and shame. The best expedient I could think of, was to creep into my house, which I accordingly did; and shutting the gate after me, I went as far as the length of my chain would suffer, and discharged my body of that uneasy load...From this time my constant practice was, as soon as I rose, to perform that business in open air, at the full extent of my chain; and due care was taken every morning before company came, that the offensive matter should be carried off in wheel-barrows, by two servants appointed for that purpose."

scenario

(sih NAIR ee oh *or* sih NAHR ee oh)

a general sketch of the plot, characters, and scenery in a dramatic work

schadenfreude

(SHAH den froi duh)

a reader's pleasure from the suffering or misfortunes of a character; from "damage joy" (German)

scop

(SKAHP)

a storyteller or minstrel from the Anglo-Saxon period; from "jester" (Old English)

semantics

(sih MAN tiks)

the study of the meanings of words and how meaning changes with the alteration of words

sentimentality

(sin tih men TAL ih tee)

an author's contrived attempt to garner emotion from the reader or audience, often from relying on affectation and shallow appeals to emotion

also referred to as being **maudlin** (MAWD lin)

[*see also* bathos]

setting

the time, place, and cultural background of a story

Examples:

> Stephen Crane's *Red Badge of Courage* is set during the Civil War.
>
> Aldous Huxley's *Brave New World* is set in a future British society.

simulacrum

(sim yuh LAY krum)

a setting, character, or object that is a superficial, inferior representation or simulation of something other; from "simulate" (Latin)

Examples of works featuring simulacra:

> *Frankenstein* (Mary Shelley)
>
> *The Picture of Dorian Gray* (Oscar Wilde)
>
> *The Adventures of Pinocchio* (Carlo Collodi)
>
> *Solaris* (Stanislaw Lem)
>
> *Jurassic Park* (Michael Crichton)

skald

a Scandinavian poet or storyteller during the period from the 9th to 13th century

also spelled **scald**

sketch

a short comic narrative; also, a brief description of a character (known as a **character sketch**)

[*see also* skit]

slang

a group of recently coined words often used in informal situations but not necessarily accepted in conventional language

Examples:

> "bling" (jewelry, particularly diamonds)
>
> "McJob" (a low-paying, uninteresting job)
>
> "pwn" (to own, or dominate, someone in a game; pronounced PONE)

[*see also* colloquialism, neologism]

snowclone

a type of cliché in which a phrase follows a formula popularized in modern culture

Examples:

In *A Hitchhiker's Guide to the Galaxy*, Douglas Adams wrote, "To boldly split infinitives that no man had split before," which is a snowclone of the well-known introduction to the *Star Trek* television series: "To boldly go where no man has gone before."

The "Got Milk" advertising campaign has spawned numerous snowclones, including "Got Jesus?" and "Got Game?"

soraismus

(sore AYS muss)

the use of different languages, either unintentionally or for humorous effect; from "to blend and mangle" (Greek)

Examples:

"The esprit de corps was muy bueno after the rendevouz with the brass."

"That game is über cool!"

soubrette

(soo BRETT)

a flirtatious and often mischievous stock female character who is the close companion or servant to the female protagonist

[*see also* ingénue]

spoonerism

when a speaker unintentionally juxtaposes letters of words (usually the initial consonants)

named after the Reverend W.A. Spooner, who was well-known for these slips

Example:

"pee little thrigs" is a spoonerism for "three little pigs"

squib

a short witty saying or humorous article in a newspaper or periodical

speaker

the one who addresses an audience; the narrator

[*see also* persona, point of view]

stereotype	a commonly held characterization or idea; a character or situation that is common and generalized
stream of consciousness	the unedited recording of a character's thoughts, which may resemble random, abstract thinking or free association also referred to as **interior (or internal) monologue**
style	the manner in which a writer conveys his or her ideas through diction, syntax, and other elements of language
sublime (sub LIME)	the aspect of grandness and excellence of or within a work; from "elevated" (Latin)
subplot	a secondary plot that is subordinate to the main action; a "plot within a plot" **Example:** Hermione Granger's efforts to liberate the house elves is a subplot of J.K. Rowling's novel *Harry Potter and the Goblet of Fire*.
subtext	the underlying meaning implicitly expressed in a literary work, particularly in a play; often expressed through character movements, pauses in dialogue, and setting
summary	a concise yet comprehensive recap of a text's essential points [*see also* paraphrase, synopsis]
suspense	the uncertainty and tension the readers or audience feels about what is going to happen next in a story **Example:** The reader may begin to feel suspense when reading the part of Elizabeth Bowen's "The Demon Lover," in which Mrs. Drover receives a mysterious letter that makes her lips "go white."

symbol

a person, place, thing, or idea that represents something else; from "to throw together" (Greek)

a **conventional symbol** is a representation whose meaning is generally universal and spans all literature

a **contextual symbol** is a representation whose meaning depends on the specific story in which it is being featured

Examples of conventional symbolism:

> fire or water for purification
> dove for peace
> a cross or fish for Christianity
> the color green for rebirth or fertility

Examples of contextual symbolism:

> the whale in Herman Melville's *Moby Dick*
> the black box in Shirley Jackson's "The Lottery"

[*see also* emblem]

---

synopsis

(sih NOP sis)

a brief summary of a work's plot or main theme

also referred to as **précis** (PRAY see **or** pray SEE)

[*see also* summary]

---

tableau

(tah BLOH)

the representation of an image by still persons or, simply, a description of still persons

---

tautology

(taw TAHL uh jee)

unnecessary repetition within a phrase or idea; saying the same thing using different words

also referred to as **redundancy**

rhetorical tautology refers to a compound proposition that is true in both instances

Examples:

> "The store offered a **free gift** to the first fifty shoppers."
> "It is shap'd, sir, like itself, and it is as broad as it has breadth. / It is just so high as it is, and moves with its own organs" (*Antony and Cleopatra*, II.vii, Shakespeare)
> **rhetorical tautology**: "Either I will go to the game, or I won't."

[*see also* parelcon, pleonasm]

---

texture	the part of a work that cannot be paraphrased without losing its core meaning or literary effect
theme	the main idea of a literary work; the thesis
thesis	the main point or theme of a work; the argument that the writer presents in an essay

effective thesis statements are focused and allow for detailed elaboration and support |
| **Tom Swifty** | an adverbial phrase that refers to an action by way of a pun

also spelled **Tom Swiftie**

Examples:
    "'Okay, okay, I did it,' said Tom admittedly."
    "'It doesn't smell anymore,' Tom said distinctly."
    "'I've been listening to those dogs all night long!' Tom barked." |
| **tone** | a general description of the overall mood of a literary work or, more specifically, an author's attitude as presented through diction, syntax, and use of literary and rhetorical devices |
| **tone shift** | a change in an author's attitude; tone may shift from paragraph to paragraph, or even from line to line |

topothesia (toh poh THEEZH yuh)	the description of an imaginary setting **Examples:**

"When I found myself on my feet, I looked about me, and must confess I never beheld a more entertaining prospect. The country around appeared like a continued garden, and the enclosed fields, which were generally forty feet square, resembled so many beds of flowers. These fields were intermingled with woods of half a stang, and the tallest trees, as I could judge, appeared to be seven feet high. I viewed the town on my left hand, which looked like the painted scene of a city in a theatre."

(*Gulliver's Travels*, Jonathan Swift)

"The island of the Utopians is two hundred miles across in the middle part where it is widest, and is nowhere much narrower than this except toward the two ends. These ends, drawn toward one another as if in a five-hundred-mile circle, make the island crescent-shaped like a new moon. Between the horns of the crescent, which are about eleven miles apart, the sea enters and spreads into a broad bay. Being sheltered from the wind by the surrounding land, the bay is never rough, but quiet and smooth instead, like a big lake. Thus, nearly the whole inner coast is one great harbor, across which ships pass in every direction to the great advantage of the people."

(*Utopia*, Sir Thomas More)

[*see also* inciuling]

univocal (yoo NIV uh kull *or* yoo nih VOH kull)	the singular meaning of a work; not having multiple or ambiguous meanings
urtext	an original version of a literary work that is lost but has been reconstructed through textual criticism
variorum edition (vair ee OR um)	a particular edition of a literary work that contains annotations and commentary
vatic (VAT ik)	a prophetic vision, particularly through an enlightened or divinely inspired storyteller or poet

verisimilitude (vair uh suh MIL uh tood)	the extent to which a literary work exhibits realism or authenticity [*see also* literary realism]
villain	a character, usually, but not always, the antagonist, of a narrative or drama, whose purpose is to complicate or destroy the lives of other characters, particularly the hero
voice	the individual writing style of a writer with respect to diction, syntax, imagery, and other elements of language
vulgate (VULL git)	the vernacular, or common language, version of a work; from "common edition" (Latin) often made in reference to *The Vulgate*, St. Jerome's Latin translation of the Holy Bible in the 14th century
willing suspension of belief	the concept by which a reader accepts the conventions of the literature or drama, including the bending of what is accepted in everyday life or the alteration of reality [*see also* poetic license]
Xanaduism (ZAN uh doo izm)	literary research that attempts to discover the sources behind works of imagination and fancy also, in a pejorative sense, refers to careless research with little care in the evaluation of sources attributed to John Livingston Lowe's book *Road to Xanadu*, which was a study of Samuel Taylor Coleridge's poem "Kubla Khan"

Xenophanic

(zee noh FAN ik)

a descriptive term that refers to wandering poets who specialize in wit and satire

named after Xenophanes, a wandering poet from Ionia (Greece) in the 6th century BCE

---

xenophobia

(zee noh FOH bee uh)

a fear or hatred of those who are different or are from another place; a key aspect of jingoism

[*see also* abjection]

Yogiism

(YOH ghee izm)

a term coined in reference to the witticisms, paradoxes, and unintentional mondegreens often made by the baseball legend Yogi Berra

Examples:

"When you come to a fork in the road, take it."
"You can observe a lot by just watching."
"It's like déjà vu all over again"
"It's not the heat, it's the humility."

[*see also* Farberism, mondegreen]

---

yonic symbol

(YON ik SIM bull)

an image or representation in literature of the female breasts or vagina; suggested interpretations have included fertility or even prolific creativity

Examples:

Often, objects that receive (metaphorically and literally) as well as items that bloom have been interpreted as yonic symbols: caves, rooms, locks, fully-bloomed roses, etc.

Dan Brown used the Holy Grail as a yonic symbol in his novel *The DaVinci Code* by equating the Grail with Mary Magdalene's womb.

[*see also* phallic symbol]

---

zoomorphism

(zoh uh MAWR fiz um)

the representation of an entity, particularly a deity, in animal form

---

assonance (ASS uh nunts)	matching vowel sounds in neighboring words without matching consonant sounds **Examples:** "Tune" and "June" are rhymes (both the vowel and consonant sounds match) "tune" and "food" are assonant (only the vowel sounds match) "Hear the mellow wedding bells," ("The Bells," Edgar Allan Poe) "Blind eyes could blaze like meteors." ("Do Not Go Gentle into That Good Night," Dylan Thomas)
alliteration (uh LIT uh RAY shun)	the repetition of the same sound at the beginning of neighboring words extreme alliteration, in which nearly every word in a line or sentence begins with the same consonant, is sometimes referred to as **paroemion** (pah ROH mee on) **Examples:** "There is always something left to love. And if you ain't learned that, you ain't learned nothing." (*A Raisin in the Sun*, Lorraine Hansberry) "Five miles meandering with a mazy motion" ("Kubla Khan," Samuel Taylor Coleridge) [*see also* assonance, consonance]
beginning rhyme	rhyme at the beginning of consecutive lines of verse; also referred to as **initial rhyme** **Example:** Mad from life's history, Glad to death's mystery. ("Bridge of Sighs," Thomas Hood)

broken rhyme	splitting a word at the end of a verse line in order to maintain rhyme; usually used for light verse

Example:

> I caught this morning morning's minion, **king-**
> **dom** of daylight's dauphin, dapple-dawn-drawn
> Falcon, in his riding
> Of the rolling level underneath him steady air, and striding
> High there, how he rung upon the rein of a wimpling **wing**
> ("The Windhover," Gerard Manley Hopkins)

cacophony (kah KOFF uh nee)	harsh discordant sounds; also referred to as **dissonance** or **jangle** opposite of euphony

Examples:

> My stick fingers click with a snicker
> And, chuckling, they knuckle the keys;
> Light footed, my steel feelers flicker
> And pluck from these keys melodies.
> ("Player Piano," James Updike)

consonance (KAHN soh nunts)	the repetition of the same consonants in a series of words

Example:

> "She broke the stick over his back until she heard a crack."

crossed rhyme	a rhyme in the middle of a line of verse that roughly corresponds to the same position in another line

Example:

> Laurel is green for a **season**, and love is sweet for a **day**;
> But love grows bitter with **treason**, and laurel outlives not **May**
> ("Hymn to Proserpine," Algernon Charles Swinburne)

end rhyme	rhyme that appears at the end of lines in verse rather than rhyme that occurs within a line of verse, which is internal rhyme

euphony (YOO fuh nee)	pleasing, harmonious sounds; the musicality in the sounds of the text; opposite of cacophony **Example:** "It lay thickly drifted on the crooked crosses and headstones, on the spears of the little gate, on the barren thorns. His soul swooned slowly as he heard the snow falling faintly through the universe and faintly falling, like the descent of their last end, upon all the living and the dead." (*Ulysses*, James Joyce)
exact rhyme	a form of rhyme in which words rhyme perfectly
eye rhyme	a kind of rhyme in which the spellings of the paired words appear to match but without a true matching of pronunciation **Examples:** "dive" and "give" "said" and "maid"

falling rhyme	rhymes that lose their emphasis in later syllables
	
	also referred to as **dying rhyme**
	
	Nelson was once Britannia's god of war,
	   And still should be so, but the tide is turn'd;
	   There 's no more to be said of Trafalgar,
	(*Don Juan*, Canto I, Lord Byron)

feminine rhyme	a rhyme on two syllables in which the first syllable is stressed and the second (or subsequent) is unstressed, unlike masculine rhyme, which has no unstressed syllables also referred to as **double rhyme** or **triple rhyme** **Examples:** "mótiŏn" / "nótiŏn" "fléeĭng" / "séeĭng" "vánĭty"/ "humánĭty"

inflection	a rise or fall of pitch in one's voice (sometimes referred to as **intonation**)
	also describes a modification of the word due to grammatical changes
internal rhyme	rhyme that occurs within a line of verse rather than rhyme that appears at the end of lines, which is end rhyme
leonine rhyme (LEE uh nine)	rhyme of a word or syllable in the middle of a line of verse with the concluding word or syllable of the same line; a type of internal rhyme

Examples:

> "Once upon a midnight **dreary**, while I pondered, weak and **weary**" ("The Raven," Edgar Allan Poe)
>
> "And the stately Spanish **men** to their flagship bore him **then**," (*The Revenge*, Alfred, Lord Tennyson)

light rhyme	when one syllable in a rhyming word is unstressed

Example:

> "O hold your tongue of your weeping," says **he**,
> "Of your weeping now let me **be**;
> I will show you how the lilies grow
> On the banks of **Italy**."
> ("The Daemon Lover," Anonymous)

masculine rhyme	a common rhyme in which the final stressed syllable of a line is the same as the final stressed syllable of another line
	also referred to as **single rhyme**

Example:

> Stand still, and I will read to **thee**
> A lecture, love, in Love's philoso**phy**.
> ("Lecture upon the Shadow," John Donne)

[*see also* feminine rhyme]

monorhyme

(MON uh rahym)

a fragment of a poem or the entire poem itself that has the same end rhyme

Example:

> All that glitters is not **gold**;
> Often have you heard that **told**:
> Many a man his life hath **sold**
> But my outside to **behold**:
> Gilded tombs do worms **enfold**.
> Had you been as wise as **bold**,
> Young in limbs, in judgment **old**,
> Your answer had not been **inscroll'd**:
> Fare you well; your suit is **cold**.
> (*Merchant of Venice*, II.vii, Shakespeare)

mosaic rhyme

(moh ZAY ik)

a rhyme spanning two or more syllables

Examples:

> "Surely Good Mrs. Murphy will demurely show goodness and mercy" (Sylvia Wright's mondegreen of Psalms 23

onomatopoeia

(ahn uh mott uh PEE uh)

a word that appears as the sound it represents; from "name making" (Greek)

Examples:

> "buzz," "crash," "whirr," "clang" "hiss," "purr," "squeak," "mumble," "hush," "boom"

phonetic intensive

(foh NET ik in TEN siv)

a sound that, to some degree, relates to the word's meaning

Examples:

an initial *gl* often accompanies the idea of light, usually unmoving, as in *glare, gleam, glint, glow,* and *glisten*

fl in a word is often associated with the idea of moving light, as in *flame, flare, flash, flicker*

sl often accompanies the idea of something being slippery and wet, as in *slippery, slick, slide, slime, slither, slop, slosh,* and *slobber, slushy*

polyphonic (pall ee FAHN ik)	having multiple, simultaneous sounds also refers to a literary work with multiple voices

rhyme	the repetition of a sound that may link one concept to another; also, an archaic term that refers to a poem in general [*see also* end rhyme, exact rhyme, eye rhyme, falling (dying) rhyme, internal rhyme, slant rhyme]

rhyme scheme	the pattern in which rhymes are arranged in a poem; often transcribed as letters representing each rhyme
	
	Example of the rhyme scheme *abab cdcd efef gg*:
	
	Let me not to the marriage of true **minds** (*a*)
	Admit impediments. Love is not **love** (*b*)
	Which alters when it alteration **finds**, (*a*)
	Or bends with the remover to **remove**: (*b*)
	O no! it is an ever-fixed **mark** (*c*)
	That looks on tempests and is never **shaken**; (*d*)
	It is the star to every wandering **bark**, (*c*)
	Whose worth's unknown, although his height be **taken**. (*d*)
	Love's not Time's fool, though rosy lips and **cheeks** (*e*)
	Within his bending sickle's compass **come**: (*f*)
	Love alters not with his brief hours and **weeks**, (*e*)
	But bears it out even to the edge of **doom**. (*f*)
	   If this be error and upon me **proved**, (*g*)
	   I never writ, nor no man ever **loved**. (*g*)
	("Sonnet 116," Shakespeare)

rime riche (reem REESH)	a rhyme that includes matching vowel sounds as well as the consonants that precede them also referred to as an **identical rhyme** **Example:** "From my head to my **sole** / I think of you as another part of my **soul**"

scarce rhyme

lines of rhyme relying on words difficult to rhyme

Example:

> But—Oh! ye lords of ladies intellectual,
> Inform us truly, have they not hen-peck'd you all?
> (*Don Juan*, Canto XXII, George Gordon, Lord Byron)

sibilance

(sib UH lentz)

repetition of "hissing" (sibilant) sounds (*s, sh, zh, c*)

sibilance is a form of **consonance**

also referred to as **sigmatism**

Example:

> Ships that pass in the night, and speak each other in passing;
> Only a signal shown and a distant voice in the darkness
> ("Tales of a Wayside Inn, 1863: Part 3," Henry Wadsworth Longfellow)

slant rhyme

a form of rhyme in which words contain similar sounds but do not rhyme perfectly

also referred to as a **approximate rhyme, half rhyme, off rhyme**, or **near rhyme**

Examples:

> "horse"/"hearse"
> "summer"/"humble"
> "thin"/"slim"

tasis

(TAY sis)

sustaining the pronunciation of a sound for the appreciation of the sound itself

Example:

> "Yummmmmmm!"
> "Euphony. The word itself sounds beautiful: eu-pho-ny."

[*see also* euphony]

thorn line	a line of verse that does not rhyme intentionally whereas other lines in the poem are rhymed

Example:

> When my devotions could not pierce
> Thy silent ears;
> Then was my heart broken, as was my verse:
> My breast was full of fears
> And **disorder**:
> ("Denial," George Herbert)

tongue twister	a sentence or phrase that is difficult to articulate quickly because of alliteration (**paroemion**) or consonance

Examples:

> "Which witch wished which wicked wish?"
> "Six sharp smart sharks."
> "Vincent vowed vengeance very vehemently."

acephalous (ey SEF uh luhs)	a line of poetry that does not have a first syllable although the meter seems to indicate a syllable should exist; also referred to as **headless rhyme** **Example:** *[First Stanza]* Thĕ tíme yŏu wón yŏur tówn thĕ ráce We chaired you through the market-place; *[Second Stanza]* **Eyés thĕ shádў níght hăs shút** Cannot see the record cut, ("To an Athlete Dying Young," Robert Houseman)
accent	stress or inflection on a syllable two variations of the accent mark are the **grave** (à) and the **acute** (á)
accentual verse	verse that has a set number of stresses in a line, irrespective of the number of syllables [*see also* accentual-syllabic verse, meter, scansion]
accentual-syllabic verse	verse that has a fixed number of stresses and syllables in each line; most common form of verse in the English language [*see also* accentual verse, meter, scansion]

acrostic

(ah KROSS tik)

a poem in which the initial letters of each line spell a name (or message)

also referred to as an **abecedarius** (ab uh sih DARE ee us)

variations on the initial pattern are

mesostich (MAY zoh stik)—using the middle letters

telestich (TELL ih stik)—using the final letters

Example:

> **A** boat beneath the sunny sky,
> **L**ingering onward dreamily
> **I**n an evening of July—
> **C**hildren three that nestle near,
> **E**ager eye and willing ear
> (*Through the Looking Glass*, Lewis Carroll)

acyron

(AK err on)

poetic license in which words are used with opposite their intended meanings; from "without authority" (Greek)

Example:

> "You are thought here to be the most / senseless and fit man for the constable of the / watch" (*Much Ado about Nothing*, III.iii, Shakespeare)

afflatus

(uh FLAY tuss)

poetic inspiration

[*see also* ligne donnée]

alexandrine

(al ig ZAN drin *or* al ig ZAN dreen)

a line of poetry consisting of six iambs

also referred to as **iambic hexameter**

Example:

> "Wíthóut ă gráve, ŭnknélled, ŭncóffĭned, ánd ŭnknówn."
> (*Childe Harold's Pilgrimage*, Lord Byron)

amphibrach

(AM fih brak)

a foot made up of three syllables, which are unstressed, stressed, and unstressed (accentual meter); or short, long, short (quantitative meter)

Examples:

> cŏnféssiŏn
> tŏgéthĕr

amphimacer

(am FIM uh ser)

a foot made up of three syllables, which are stressed, unstressed, and stressed (accentual meter); or long, short, long (quantitative meter)

also referred to as a **cretic foot**

Examples:

"Soúnd thĕ Flúte! / Nów ĭt's múte." ("Spring," William Blake)

[*see also* amphibrach]

---

anacrusis

(an uh KROO sis)

an unstressed syllable (or syllables) that begins a line of verse but is not counted as part of the actual meter of the line

Example:

"**Frŏm** ráinbŏw cloúds thĕre flów nŏt" ("To a Skylark," Percy Shelley)

---

anapest

(ANN uh pest)

a metrical foot made up of two unstressed syllables followed by a stressed syllable (as in the word ĭntĕrrúpt)

Example:

"Nŏt ă wórd tŏ eăch óthĕr; wĕ képt thĕ greăt páce / Neck by neck, stride by stride, never changing our place." ("How They Brought the Good News from Ghent to Aix," Robert Browning)

---

antiphon

(AN tuh fon)

song or verse chanted or sung in response to each other in alternating stanzas

[*see also* hymn]

---

ars poetica

(ARZ poh ET ih kuh)

a discussion concerning the art and conventions of poetry

ballad (BAL ud)	a narrative poem, usually simple and short, that is meant to be sung a **folk ballad** is one that has been passed down orally from generation to generation, often telling a tale of true love but involving some element of sadness **literary ballads**, on the other hand, are composed in a formal manner in a contemporary sense, a ballad also generally refers to a pop, country, or modern rock love song **Example:** *Rime of the Ancient Mariner* (Samuel Taylor Coleridge)
ballade (buh LAHD)	a style of poetry popular in 14th and 15th century France that consists of three eight-line stanzas with the rhyme scheme ***ababbcbc*** and a four-line envoi with the rhyme scheme ***bcbc***
ballad meter	quatrain that alternates four stresses in the first and third lines and three stresses in the second and fourth lines, usually with the rhyme scheme ***abcb*** [*see also* common measure]
blank verse	unrhymed iambic pentameter **Example:** Though chang'd in outward lustre; that fixt mind And high disdain, from sence of injur'd merit, That with the mightiest rais'd me to contend, And to the fierce contention brought along Innumerable force of Spirits arm'd That durst dislike his reign, and me preferring, His utmost power with adverse power oppos'd In dubious Battel on the Plains of Heav'n, And shook his throne. What though the field be lost? All is not lost; the unconquerable Will, And study of revenge, immortal hate, And courage never to submit or yield. (*Paradise Lost*, Book I, John Milton)

blazon

(BLAY zun)

a literary device used frequently in Petrarchan sonnets in which the poet details a woman's physical attributes

Example:

> In whose each part all pens may dwell?
> Her hair fine threads of finest gold
> In curled knots man's thought to hold;
> But that her forehead says, 'in me
> A whiter beauty you may see."
> Whiter indeed; more white than snow
> Which on cold winter's face doth grow.
>
> ....
>
> Her cheeks with kindly claret spread,
> Aurora-like new out of bed,
> Or like the fresh queen-apple's side,
> Blushing at sight of Phoebus' pride.
> Her nose, her chin, pure ivory wears,
> No purer than the pretty ears,
> Save that therein appears some blood,
> Like wine and milk that mingled stood.
> ("What tongue can her perfections tell?" Sir Philip Sidney)

parodied by some poets as a **contreblazon** (KAHN truh BLAY zun)

Example:

> My mistress' eyes are nothing like the sun;
> Coral is far more red than her lips' red:
> If snow be white, why then her breasts are dun;
> If hairs be wires, black wires grow on her head.
> I have seen roses damask'd, red and white,
> But no such roses see I in her cheeks;
> And in some perfumes is there more delight
> Than in the breath that from my mistress reeks.
> I love to hear her speak,--yet well I know
> That music hath a far more pleasing sound;
> I grant I never saw a goddess go,
> My mistress when she walks, treads on the ground;
> And yet, by heaven, I think my love as rare
> As any she belied with false compare.
> ("Sonnet 130," Shakespeare)

[*see also* effictio]

bob and wheel	a metrical device used in Middle English poetry in which the first line (the bob) is very short and contains one or two stresses, and the successive lines (the wheel) are longer and contain three stresses each

frequently used in the Pearl Poet's *Sir Gawain and the Green Knight*

Example:

On mony bonkkes ful brode Bretayn he settes
with wynne,
    Where werre and wrake and wonder
    Bi sythes has wont therinne,
    And oft bothe blysse and blunder
    Ful skete has skyfted synne.
[The line "with wynne" is the bob, and the four successive lines are the wheel.]
(*Sir Gawain and the Green Knight*, Pearl Poet)

burden	a refrain or repeated chorus of a song, sometimes appearing at the beginning and separate from the stanzas

Burns stanza	a six line stanza with the rhyme scheme ***aaabab***; the first, second, third, and fifth line are tetrameters and the fourth and sixth lines are dimeters

also referred to as **Burns meter** or **Scottish stanza**

Example:

O THOU! whatever title suit thee—
Auld Hornie, Satan, Nick, or Clootie,
Wha in yon cavern grim an' sootie,
Clos'd under hatches,
Spairges about the brunstane cootie,
To scaud poor wretches!
("Address to the Devil," Robert Burns)

caesura (see ZHOOR uh)	a space in a line of verse that indicates a pause **Example:**

Who bears it, knows   what a bitter companion,
Shoulder to shoulder,   sorrow can be,
("The Wanderer," Anonymous)

carol

a joyful song of worship or celebration

catalectic

(kat uh LEK tik)

a line of verse that does not have part of the last metrical foot; from "to leave off the end" (Greek)

also referred to as **catalexis** or **truncation**

Example:

Ín thĕ góldĕn líghtnĭng *(six feet)*
óf thĕ súnkĕn sún, *(five feet)*
O'er which clouds are bright'ning, *(six feet)*
Thou dost float and run *(five feet)*
("To a Skylark," Percy Shelley)

choriambus

(kore ee AM bus)

a metrical foot that combines trochee and iamb; often used in combination with other more standard metrical feet

also referred to as **choriamb**

Example:

"Whát swĕet vĭsión óf sleĕp lurĕd thée áwăy, dŏwn fróm thé líght ăbóve?" ("Choriambics," Charles Swinburne)

chant royal

(SHAHN roi AL)

five stanzas of eleven ten-syllable lines with the rhyme scheme ***ababccddede***, followed by an envoi with the rhyme scheme ***ddede***; there is a refrain that occurs in each of the stanzas and envoi

cheville

(shuh VEE)

a word or phrase used in a line of verse to insert the necessary number of syllables for the intended meter to work; from "plug" (French)

Example:

"**Fŏr sóthe**, Ĭ táke ăl thát mĕn wól mĕ yíve"
["For sothe" is added to make the line an iambic pentameter]
(*The Canterbury Tales*, Chaucer)

cinquain

(sin KANE)

a five-line stanza, usually with the rhyme scheme *ababb*

Example:

> Murmuring how she loved me – she
> Too weak, for all her heart endeavor,
> To set its struggling passion free
> From pride, and vainer ties dissever,
> And give herself to me for ever
> ("Porphyria's Lover," Robert Browning)

clerihew

(KLER uh hyoo)

a witty four-line poem composed of two couplets, irregular in length, that contain a rhyme using a name

Example:

> Sir Humphry Davy
> Was not fond of gravy
> He lived in the odium
> Of having discovered sodium
> (Edmund Clerihew Bentley)

closed couplet

two lines of rhyming verse within a poem that can be self-contained and can have meaning independent of the larger work

Example:

> True Wit is Nature to advantage dress'd,
> What oft was thought, but ne'er so well express'd;
> (*Essay on Criticism*, Alexander Pope)

[*see also* distich]

closed form

refers to poetry that is composed using fixed, established patterns of meter, line length, syntax, or rhyme

examples include sonnets, villanelles, sestinas, haiku, and any other poem type that has an established pattern

also referred to as **fixed form**

[*see also* open form]

common measure	a quatrain that alternates four stresses in the first and third lines and three stresses in the second and fourth lines, usually with the rhyme scheme ***abab***
	also referred to as **common meter** or **hymnal stanza**
	[*see also* ballad meter]

complaint	a poem of complaint about fickle or absent love or concern over the state of affairs in the world

Examples:

> *A Complaint unto Pity* (Chaucer)
> *Complaint of Chaucer to His Purse* (Chaucer)
> *The Ruines of Time* (Edmund Spenser)

concrete poetry	a poem that forms an image through the printed text
	sometimes referred to as **pattern poetry**, **picture poetry**, **shape poetry**, or **emblem poetry**

Examples:

> Michael McFee's poem "In Medias Res" features gradually increasing line lengths from the beginning to the middle of the poem and then gradually decreasing line lengths from the middle to the end, giving the effect of a large middle section.
>
> Guillaume Apollinaire's poem "Il pleut," a poem about rain, is written in the shape of rainfall.

conversation poem	blank verse poetry attributed to Samuel Taylor Coleridge to convey pensiveness and purpose

Examples:

> "The Nightingale: A Conversation Poem" (Samuel Taylor Coleridge)
>
> "This Lime-Tree Bower My Prison" (Samuel Taylor Coleridge)

couplet (CUP let)	a pair of rhyming verse lines, usually of the same length

Example:

> But thou art all my art, and dost advance
> As high as learning my rude ignorance
> ("Sonnet 78," Shakespeare)

[*see also* distich]

Cowleyan ode
 	
(KOW lee un)
	an ode that has irregular line length, meter, and rhyme and often appears in verse groups of unequal length and irregular structure
	
	attributed to 17th century poet Abraham Cowley, who used the form regularly
	
	Examples:
	
	    Death of the Duke of Wellington (Alfred, Lord Tennyson)
	    Intimations of Immortality (William Wordsworth)
	    "Ode. Of Wit" (Abraham Cowley)

attributed to 17th century poet Abraham Cowley, who used the form regularly

crown	in the literary sense, a sequence of lyric poems in which the last line of each poem begins the next poem in sequence, and the last line of the last poem in the sequence repeats the first line in the first poem of the sequence

cycle	a group of narrative poems that share a common subject [*see also* crown, saga]

dactyl
 	
(DAK till)
	a metrical foot consisting of one stressed syllable followed by two unstressed syllables (as in *pórtăblĕ* or *márgĭnăl*)
	
	the adjective form is **dactylic** (dak TILL ik)
	
	Examples:
	
	    "Pát-ă-căke, Pát-ă-căke"
	    "Cánnŏn ĭn / frónt ŏf thĕm" ("The Charge of the Light Brigade," Alfred, Lord Tennyson)

débat (DAY bah)	a type of poem, popular in the Middle Ages, that features two personas representing conflicting values **Example:** "The Owl and the Nightingale" (Anonymous)

defective foot	a metrical foot that is incomplete, lacking one or more of its unstressed syllables

Example:

"Stánd lĭke Drúĭds ŏf éld," ("Evangeline," Henry Wadsworth Longfellow)

demotion	the use of a stressed syllable in a normally unstressed part of a metrical foot in order to vary or slow the rhythm

diamante (dee uh mahn TAY)	poetry that is arranged in a diamond pattern using seven lines and written according the specifications outlined below; from "diamond" (Middle French)

line 1—one word subject consisting of a noun

line 2—two adjectives describing the subject in line one

line 3—three participles (*–ing* or *–ed* ending) describing the subject in line one

line 4—four words, consisting of two words related to the subject in line one and two words related to the subject in line seven

line 5—three participles (*–ing* or *–ed* ending) describing the subject in line seven

line 6—two adjectives describing the subject in line seven

line 7—one word subject that contrasts with subject in line one

Example:

Peace
Calm, tranquil
Embracing, understanding, sharing
Harmony, accord, disagreement, battle
Fighting, sparring, struggling
Crusade, skirmish
War

diastole

(dahy ASS tull ee)

the lengthening of a syllable sound or shifting of an accent to accommodate meter

Examples:

"Ĭ knŏw thĕe wéll: ă sérvĭceáblĕ víllaĭn;" (*King Lear*, IV.vi, Shakespeare)

"Ănd pówĕr, úntŏ ítsĕlf móst cŏmméndáblĕ," (*Coriolanus*, IV.vii, Shakespeare)

[*see also* systole]

---

dimeter

(DIM uh turr)

a line of verse consisting of two metrical feet

Example:

"Thĕ clóck strŭck óne / Ănd dówn hĕ rán"

---

dipody

(DIP oh dee)

the combination of two metrical feet

also referred to as **syzygy** (SIZ ih jee)

---

distich

(DIS tik)

a self-contained couplet; two lines of rhyming verse that is separate unto itself or has meaning independent from the entire work

a type of closed couplet

---

dizain

(dee ZEHN)

French verse consisting of ten lines with ten syllables each, often rhyming *ababbccded*

frequently used in 15th and 16th century verse as a stanza preceding a **ballade** or **chant royal**

---

doggerel

(DOG uh rell)

rough, loosely written comic verse

Example:

"A bit of talcum / Is always walcum." ("Ode to Baby," Ogden Nash)

---

dolce stil nuovo

(DOLE chay still noo OH voh)

a literary style of poetry from 13th century Italy featuring a sophisticated use of literary devices and a focus on female beauty; from "sweet new style" (Italian)

---

dramatic monologue a poem in which a single narrator (not the poet but rather his or her persona) addresses an imaginary audience and reveals intimate personal feelings and emotions

Examples:

> *The Love Song of Alfred J. Prufrock* (T.S. Eliot)
> "Ulysses" (Alfred, Lord Tennyson)

dramatic poetry any drama that is written as poetry to be spoken

also referred to as **dramatic verse** and **dramatic lyric**

Examples:

> *A Midsummer Night's Dream* (Shakespeare)
> *Idylls of the King* (Alfred, Lord Tennyson)
> *The Love-Song of J. Alfred Prufrock* (T.S. Eliot)

dub poetry a late 20th century style of lyric poetry originating in Jamaica, as well as England, that focuses on themes of injustice, sex, and Rastafarianism

duple meter

(DOO puhl)

a metrical foot consisting of two syllables; an iamb (*ŭntó*) or a trochee (*chórŭs*)

[*see also* triple meter]

eclogue

(EKK log)

a poem (particularly pastoral) written in dialogue form

elegiac couplet

(el uh JAY ik KUP let)

two lines of verse frequently used in Greek and Latin poetry and rarely in English

the first line of the couplet contains a dactylic hexameter, and the second line contains a dactylic pentameter

also referred to as **elegiac distich**

the meter used in the elegiac couplet is called **elegiac meter**

Examples:

> Odi et amo. quare id faciam, fortasse requiris?
> nescio, sed fieri sentio et excrucior.
> ("Odi et Amo," Catullus)

> In the hexameter rises the fountain's silvery column:
> In the pentameter aye falling in melody back
> ("The Ovidian Elegiac Metre," Samuel Taylor Coleridge)

end-stopped line

a poetic expression in which the completion of a phrase, clause, or sentence coincides with the end of each line; thus, the meaning or sense of the line is complete within itself (as opposed to enjambment)

Example:

> I was angry with my friend:
> I told my wrath, my wrath did end.
> I was angry with my foe:
> I told it not, my wrath did grow.
> ("A Poison Tree," William Blake)

enjambment

a poetic expression that spans more than one line; the completion of a phrase, clause, or sentence is held over to the following line so that the line ending is not emphasized (as opposed to an end-stopped line); from "striding over" (French)

also referred to as a **run-on line**

Example:

> It is a beauteous evening, calm and free,
> The holy time is quiet as a Nun
> Breathless with adoration; the broad sun
> Is sinking down in its tranquility
> ("Evening on Calais Beach," William Wordsworth)

---

envelope

a line or stanza that is repeated in poetry; the repetition can be either identical or with some variation

Example:

> Tyger! Tyger! burning bright
> In the forests of the night,
> What immortal hand or eye
> Dare frame thy fearful symmetry?
> [these lines are repeated in William Blake's "The Tyger" as the first and final stanzas]

[*see also* refrain]

---

envoi

(AHN voi *or* EN voi)

a half syllable that occurs at the end of a ballade or chant royal

---

epigone

(EPP ih gohn)

a less respectable or otherwise inferior imitator of a greater author or poet

[*see also* poetaster]

---

epithalamion

(epp ih thuh LAY mee ahn)

a lyric poem meant to celebrate a wedding

Example:

> "Epithalamion" (Edmund Spenser)

epyllion
 	
(eh PILL ee on)
	a lyric narrative that shares many of the conventions of a fully developed epic poem but not the length
	Examples:
	
	    Hero and Leander (Christopher Marlowe)
	    Venus and Adonis (Shakespeare)

erasure poetry	poetry that is created by deleting words from an existing text and recasting what is left over into verse form a type of **found poem**
falling rhythm	when a line of verse is more accented toward the beginning, usually with trochaic and dactylic meters also referred to as **descending rhythm**
feminine ending	a line of verse ending with an extra unstressed syllable also referred to as a **light ending** **Example:** "Tŏ bé ŏr nót tŏ bé, thăt ís thĕ quéstiŏn" (*Hamlet*, III.i, Shakespeare) [*see also* hypercatalectic, weak ending]
fit	an archaic term used to denote a division of a long poem [*see also* canto]
flyting (FLAHYT ing)	a verbal conflict between two poets or two characters within a poem
foot	a measure of rhythm by which a line of poetry is divided the five most common types of feet are **iamb**, **trochee**, **anapest**, **dactyl**, and **spondee**

found poem	poetry that is composed of lines and sentences from separate sources and juxtaposed together; a collage of sorts

Example:

> Amelia was just fourteen and out of the orphan asylum; at her
>   first job--in the bindery, and yes sir, yes ma'am, oh, so
>   anxious to please.
> She stood at the table, her blond hair hanging about her
>   shoulders, "knocking up" for Mary and Sadie, the stichers
> [from *Testimony* (Charles Reznikoff), created from snippets of
>   various law reports]

[*see also* erasure poetry]

four meanings	a term advanced by critic I.A. Richards to identify four types of meaning in a poem:

- **sense**—what is said
- **feeling**—poet's emotional attitude
- **tone**—poet's attitude toward audience
- **intention**—poet's purpose, intended effect

free verse	unrhymed poetry with irregular meter and varied line lengths

also referred to as **vers libre** (vurss LEE bray)

Example:

> in the quiver on Paris's back the head
> of the arrow for Achilles' heel
> smiled in its sleep
> ("The Judgment of Paris," W.S. Merwin)

goliardic verse (gall ee ARE dik)	poetry written during the 12th and 13th centuries by a wandering band of poets that celebrated sensuality and gluttony and satirized the clergy

graveyard poetry	18th century poetry featuring gloomy imagery and themes preoccupied with death; often set in graveyards

18th century poetry featuring gloomy imagery and themes preoccupied with death; often set in graveyards

Examples:

"Elegy Written in a Country Churchyard" (Thomas Gray)
"A Night-Piece on Death" (Thomas Parnell)

---

haiku

(hahy KOO)

a Japanese verse form consisting of three unrhymed lines that together contain a total of seventeen syllables (typically consisting of five, seven, and five syllables respectively)

haiku poetry typically uses nature as its subject, using associations and suggestion to appeal to emotion and to generate a moment of spiritual awareness or discovery

also referred to as **hokku**

Example:

I am nobody:
A red sinking autumn sun
Took my name away.
("Five Haikus," Richard Wright)

---

hemistich

(HIM ih stik)

a half-line of verse, either separated from the rest of a line with a caesura or standing as a line by itself; from "half line" (Greek)

Example:

Who bears it, knows   what a bitter companion,
Shoulder to shoulder,   sorrow can be,
("The Wanderer," Anonymous)

---

hendecasyllabic

(hen dek uh sih LAH bik)

a line of verse that has eleven syllables

---

heptameter

(hep TAM uh turr)

a line of verse that contains seven metrical feet

often referred to as a **septenary** or **fourteener**

Example:

"'Tĭs bút ăs ívў̆-leáves ăroúnd thĕ rúĭn'd túrrĕt wréathe,"
("Youth and Age," Lord Byron)

heroic couplet
 	
(hih ROH ik CUP let)
	a pair of rhymed lines (couplet) written in iambic pentameter
	
	Chaucer was the first poet to use heroic couplets
	
	also referred to as a **riding rhyme**
	Example:
	    Meanwhile, declining from the noon of day,
	    The sun obliquely shoots his burning ray;
	    The hungry judges soon the sentence sign,
	    And wretches hang that jurymen may dine. . . .
	    (two couplets from Alexander Pope's *The Rape of the Lock*)
	
	[*see also* brachyology]

heroic quatrain
 	
(hih ROH ik KWAH trane)
	four lines of alternating rhymed lines of iambic pentameter (***abab***)
	
	also referred to as a **heroic stanza** or **elegiac stanza**
	Example:
	    Far from the madding crowd's ignoble strife,
	    Their sober wishes never learn'd to stray;
	    Along the cool sequester'd vale of life
	    They kept the noiseless tenour of their way.
	    ("Elegy Written in a Country Churchyard," Thomas Gray)

hexameter (heks AM ih turr)	a line of verse that contains six metrical feet
hexastich (HEKS ih stik)	a six-line stanza; from "six lines" (Greek)
homostrophic (hoh moh STROH fik)	a repeated stanza form in rhyme scheme, length, and meter
Horatian ode (hoh RAY shun)	an ode that has the same meter and rhyme in each of its stanzas; named after the Roman poet Horace

hovering stress

an accent on a syllable that may or may not be needed but is not specified

also referred to as **hovering accent** or **distributed stress**

Hudibrastic verse

(hew dih BRASS tik)

a term derived from Samuel Butler's *Hudibras* to describe octosyllabic comic verse in couplet form, often using feminine rhyme

Example:

> When civil dudgeon first grew high,
> And men fell out they knew not why?
> When hard words, jealousies, and fears,
> Set folks together by the ears,
> And made them fight, like mad or drunk,
> For Dame Religion, as for punk;
> Whose honesty they all durst swear for,
> Though not a man of them knew wherefore:
> When Gospel-Trumpeter, surrounded
> With long-ear'd rout, to battle sounded,
> And pulpit, drum ecclesiastick,
> Was beat with fist, instead of a stick;
> Then did Sir Knight abandon dwelling,
> And out he rode a colonelling.
> ("The Puritan," *Hudibras*, Samuel Butler)

huitain

(WEE tehn)

French verse form consisting of eight lines with eight-to ten syllables per line

the rhyme scheme is usually *ababbcbc* or *abbaacac*

hypercatalectic

(hahy purr kat ih LEK tik)

a line of verse that has an extra syllable at the end; from "beyond the last foot" (Greek)

also referred to as **hypermetrical**

Example:

> Ĭ thríce prĕséntĕd hím ă kíngly̆ crówn
> Whĭch hé dĭd thríce rĕfúse. Wăs thís ămbítiŏn?
> [the second line is hypercatalectic]
> (*Julius Caesar*, III.ii, Shakespeare)

iamb

a metrical foot consisting of an unstressed syllable followed by a stressed syllable (as in *rĕspéct*)

the iamb is the most common metrical foot in English poetry

the adjective form is **iambic** (eye AM bik)

Example:

Ă slúmbĕr díd mў spírĭt seál;
I had no human fears:
("A Slumber Did My Spirit Seal," William Wordsworth)

---

iambic pentameter

(ahy AM bik pen TAM ih turr)

a line of verse made up of five iambs

Example:

"Bĕyónd thĕ útmŏst bou̇nd ŏf húmăn thou̇ght." ("Ulysses," Alfred, Lord Tennyson)

---

ictus

(IK tuss)

a stress or accent mark placed on a syllable in a line of verse; from "stroke" (Latin)

In Memoriam stanza

(in muh MORE ee um)

a four-line iambic tetrameter with the rhyme scheme *abba*

derives its name from its use in Alfred, Lord Tennyson's poem *In Memoriam*

Example:

Knŏwn ánd ŭnknówn; hŭmán, dĭvíne;
Sweet human hand and lips and eye;
Dear heavenly friend that canst not die,
Mine, mine, for ever, ever mine;
(*In Memoriam*, Alfred, Lord Tennyson)

incremental repetition	a repetition of one or more lines, with some variation, in a ballad, usually to move the action forward

Example:

'O good Lord Judge, and sweet Lord Judge,
Peace for a little while!
Methinks I see my own father,
Come riding by the stile.
'Oh father, oh father, a little of your gold,
And likewise of your fee!
To keep my body from yonder grave,
And my neck from the gallows-tree.'
'None of my gold now you shall have,
Nor likewise of my fee;
For I am come to see you hangd,
And hanged you shall be.'
'O good Lord Judge, and sweet Lord Judge,
Peace for a little while!
Methinks I see my own mother,
Come riding by the stile.
'Oh mother, oh mother, a little of your gold,
And likewise of your fee,
To keep my body from yonder grave,
And my neck from the gallows-tree!'
'None of my gold now shall you have,
Nor likewise of my fee;
For I am come to see you hangd,
And hanged you shall be.'
(*Ballads,* "Number 95: The Maid Freed from the Gallows," Francis Child)

jingle	a catchy line of verse (either through rhyme, meter, or musicality) usually intended for product advertisements

Examples:

"Plop-plop, Fizz-fizz. Oh, what a relief it is!" (Alka-Seltzer antacid tablets)

"You deserve a break today!" (McDonalds restaurants)

"Sometimes you feel like a nut; sometimes you don't. Almond Joy's got nuts; Mounds don't." (Almond Joy and Mounds candy bars, The Hershey Company)

kenning	a compound word or phrase used in Old English verse to represent something else
	Examples:
	"whale-road" for "sea"
	"oar-steed" for "ship"

lai	short narrative verse originating from medieval France
(LAY)	features stories of chivalry and true love, often incorporating supernatural elements, particularly of the mythical fairy world; written in eight syllable lines and meant to be sung
	sometimes referred to as a **Breton lay** or **narrative lay**
	also spelled **lay**
	Examples:
	"Sir Gowther" (Anonymous)
	"Lai le Freine" (Anonymous)

level stress	when two adjacent syllables have equal stress
	also referred to as **even accent**
	[*see also* hovering stress]

ligne donnée	a term used by the poet Paul Valéry to describe a line of poetry that a poet receives through divine inspiration or a muse; from "given line" (French)
(leeg NAY don NAY)	[*see also* afflatus]

light verse	verse that does not have a serious tone; generally regarded for accomplished rhyming patterns
	[*see also* doggerel, limerick]

limerick	a short, humorous (sometimes coarse) poem that consists of five lines rhyming ***aabba***

Example:

> There was an Old Man with a beard,
> Who said, "It is just as I feared!
> Two Owls and a Hen,
> Four Larks and a Wren,
> Have all built their nests in my beard!"
> (*A Book of Nonsense*, Edward Lear)

lyric poetry	a short, musical poem intended to convey feelings or emotions as opposed to telling a story

Examples:

> "Kubla Khan" (Samuel Taylor Coleridge)
> "Tintern Abbey" (William Wordsworth)
> "Dover Beach" (Matthew Arnold)

[*see also* dramatic poetry, narrative poetry]

macaronic verse (MAK uh rahn ik)	poetry that contains lines of verse using more than one language

Example:

> In happy homes he saw the light
> Of household fires gleam warm and bright;
> Above, the spectral glaciers shone,
> And from his lips escaped a groan,
> **Excelsior!**
>
> "Try not the Pass!" the old man said:
> "Dark lowers the tempest overhead,
> The roaring torrent is deep and wide!
> And loud that clarion voice replied,
> **Excelsior!**
> ("Excelsior," Henry Wadsworth Longfellow)

madrigal (MAD drih gull)	a short lyric poem that focuses on country life or love and set to music with vocal accompaniment; from "simple living; maternal" (Latin)

meter	the measurement of the rhythm established by a poem
	meter is usually dependent not only on the number of syllables in a line but also on the way those syllables are accented

Miltonic sonnet (mill TAHN ik SAHN it)	a sonnet form designed by the English poet John Milton that resembles a Petrarchan sonnet by form and rhyme scheme but does not contain a turn at the beginning of the second stanza

monometer (muh NAHM uh turr)	one metrical foot in a line of verse **Example:** 　"Soúnd thĕ Flúte! / Nów ĭt's múte." 　("Spring," William Blake)

monostich (MAHN oh stik)	a poem consisting of one line or referring to a single line of verse; from "one line" (Greek)

narrative poetry	a story told in verse form **Examples:** 　*The Canterbury Tales* (Chaucer) 　"The Charge of the Light Brigade" (Alfred, Lord Tennyson) 　*The Divine Comedy* (Dante) 　*Metamorphoses* (Ovid)

nonsense verse	light, humorous poetry that uses meaningless words or confusing ideas

Examples:

'Twas brillig, and the slithy toves
Did gyre and gimble in the wabe;
All mimsy were the borogoves,
And the mome raths outgrabe.
("Jabberwocky," Lewis Carroll)

The Owl and the Pussycat went to sea
In a beautiful pea green boat,
They took some honey, and plenty of money,
Wrapped up in a five pound note.
("The Owl and the Pussycat," Edward Lear)

octave (AHK tiv)	an eight line stanza; the first stanza in a Petrarchan sonnet

octosyllabic (OK toh sih LAB ik)	a line of verse written in iambic or trochaic tetrameter (eight syllables), often used in couplets

Example:

Thĕse pléasŭres Mélănchólў gíve,
And I with thee will choose to live.
(*Il Penseroso*, John Milton)

Old English versification	the metrical structure often used in recited verse (oral literature) during the Anglo-Saxon period composed of two half-lines (hemistichs) separated by a pause (caesura) and often connected through alliteration

Example:

Hwæt! We Gardena   in geardagum,
þeodcyninga,   þrym gefrunon,
hu ða æþelingas   ellen fremedon.
Oft Scyld Scefing   sceaþena þreatum
(*Beowulf*, Anonymous)

open form	poetry that does not have an established pattern in meter, rhyme, line length, or syntax

Example:

> POETS to come! orators, singers, musicians to come!
> Not to-day is to justify me, and answer what I am for;
> But you, a new brood, native, athletic, continental, greater than before known,
> Arouse! Arouse—for you must justify me—you must answer.
>
> I myself but write one or two indicative words for the future,
> I but advance a moment, only to wheel and hurry back in the darkness.
>
> I am a man who, sauntering along, without fully stopping, turns a casual look upon you, and then averts his face,
> Leaving it to you to prove and define it,
> Expecting the main things from you.
> ("Poets to Come," *Leaves of Grass*, Walt Whitman)

[*see also* closed form, free verse]

ottava rima (oh TAHV uh REE mah)	an eight-line stanza (**octave**) written in iambic pentameter with the rhyme scheme ***abababcc***

Example:

> They looked up to the sky, whose floating glow
> Spread like a rosy ocean, vast and bright;
> They gazed upon the glittering sea below,
> Whence the broad moon rose circling into sight;
> They heard the waves splash, and the wind so low,
> And saw each other's dark eyes darting light
> Into each other—and, beholding this,
> Their lips drew near, and clung into a kiss.
> (*Don Juan*, Lord Byron)

paeon (PEE on)	in quantitative verse, a metrical foot consisting of three unstressed syllables and one stressed syllable

palinode (PAL uh node)	a lyric or ode meant to retract an earlier statement or viewpoint; from "singing back" (Greek) **Example:** A prominent example is provided by the poet Stesichorus in which he disavows an earlier statement that Helen of Troy had chosen Paris over Menelaus: The story is not true, She never went in the well-decked ships, She didn't travel to the towers of Troy.
parnassian (par NASS ee un)	a term either relating to poetry in general or specifically to the style of 19th century French poetry that is emotionally detached and metrically precise
pastourelle (pass toh RELL)	an Old French lyric pastoral poem form popular in Medieval Europe that features a knight recounting his attempts to seduce a simple shepherdess
pentameter (pen TAM uh turr)	five metrical feet in a line of verse **Example:** "Běyónd thě útmŏst boúnd ŏf húmăn thoúght." ("Ulysses," Alfred, Lord Tennyson)

Petrarchan sonnet (puh TRAHR kun)	a fourteen line sonnet consisting of two parts: the octave, eight lines with the rhyme scheme ***abbaabba***, and the sestet, six lines usually with the rhyme scheme ***cdecde***
	the octave often poses a question or dilemma that the sestet answers or resolves, beginning with a **turn**, also known as a **volta**
	also referred to as an **Italian sonnet**

Example:

> Whoso list to hunt, I know where is an hind!
> But as for me, alas, I may no more;
> The vain travail hath wearied me so sore,
> I am of them that furthest come behind.
> Yet may I by no means my wearied mind
> Draw from the deer, but as she fleeth afore
> Fainting I follow; I leave off therefore,
> Since in a net I seek to hold the wind.
>
> Who list her hunt, I put him out of doubt,
> As well as I, may spend his time in vain.
> And graven with diamonds in letters plain,
> There is written her fair neck round about,
> "Noli me tangere, for Caesar's I am,
> And wild for to hold, though I seem tame.
> ("Whoso List to Hunt," Thomas Wyatt)

plaintive poetry	verse that expresses grief or sadness [*see also* elegy, eulogy]

poet laureate (POH et LORE ee it)	a title of distinction given to the official poet of a nation or kingdom

poetaster (POH it ass turr)	a label applied to a poet with little skill or literary regard from his or her peers [*see also* epigone]

poetic diction	the specific word choice and style used in poetry, particularly that which is not used in prose; often suggests ornamental, figurative, and, sometimes, archaic language [*see also* poeticism]
poeticism (poh ET eh sizm)	diction, usually archaic, that is generally used only for poetry **Examples:** "o'er," "doth," and "bestride" [*see also* archaism, poetic diction]
poetry	a literary work written in verse form in which rhythmic language and syntax, as well as literary and sound devices, are used for effect; from "making" or "creating" (Greek)

poulter's measure	a rhyming couplet consisting of an iambic hexameter (alexandrine) and an iambic heptameter (fourteener); frequently used in morality plays and 16th century poetry
	Example:
	   So feeble is the thread that doth the burden stay
	    Of my poor life, in heavy plight that falleth in decay,
	   (Sir Thomas Wyatt)

prose poetry	a work distinguished as prose but having the conventions of poetry, such as ornate, rhythmic language and the incorporation of rhyme and other sound devices notable writers of this type include T.S. Eliot, Amy Lowell, and Oscar Wilde
prosody (PRAHZ uh dee)	the analysis and study of versification (including elements such as form, meter, and rhyme) [*see also* scansion]

pyrrhic

(PEER ik)

a metrical foot consisting of two unaccented syllables; a pyrrhic foot is extremely rare in English poetry

also referred to as a **dibrach**

Example:

"Ĭ hăve beĕn proúd ănd sáid, 'Mў lóve, mў ówn.'"

[the first two syllables from Elizabeth Browning's *Sonnets from the Portuguese* contain a pyrrhic foot, followed by four iambic feet]

---

quantitative verse

the categorization of meter according to syllable length rather than on stresses; used frequently in Latin and Greek poetry but rarely in English poetry

---

quatrain

(KWAH trane)

a stanza containing four lines

also referred to as a **tetrastich** (TEH truh stik)

---

refrain

(ree FRAYN)

lines that recur throughout a poem or lyrics of a song

Example:

"She said, 'I am aweary, aweary, / I would that I were dead.'"

[every stanza but the last in Alfred, Lord Tennyson's "Mariana" concludes with the preceding two-line refrain]

[*see also* envelope]

---

repetend

(rep ih TEND *or* REP ih tend)

a syllable, word, or line of verse that is repeated at irregular intervals throughout a poem

[*see also* refrain]

---

reverdie

(rev er DEE)

a poem that celebrates the arrival of spring

---

rhyme royal (RIME roi AL)	a seven line poem written in iambic pentameter that has the rhyme scheme ***ababbcc*** also referred to as a **Chaucerian stanza** **Example:** The double sorwe of Troilus to tellen, That was the king Priamus sone of Troye, In lovinge, how his aventures fellen Fro wo to wele, and after out of Ioye, My purpos is, er that I parte fro ye. Thesiphone, thou help me for tendyte Thise woful vers, that wepen as I wryte! (*Troilus and Criselde*, Chaucer)
rhythm	a pattern of stressed and unstressed syllables; the "beat" of a work, often expressed as **cadence** (KAY dens), the rising and falling of the rhythm
rising rhythm	when unstressed syllables are linked with stressed syllables that follow rather than precede them

rondel

(RON dull)

a verse form similar to the French **rondeau**

composed of thirteen to fourteen lines, with a two-line refrain that opens the rondel and reappears as lines seven and eight (the rhyme scheme is usually ***ABba abAB abbaA***)

not to be confused with the roundel

Example:

> Your two great eyes will slay me suddenly;
> Their beauty shakes me who was once serene;
> Straight through my heart the wound is quick and keen.
>
> Only your word will heal the injury
> To my hurt heart, while yet the wound is clean -
> Your two great eyes will slay me suddenly;
> Their beauty shakes me who was once serene.
>
> Upon my word, I tell you faithfully
> Through life and after death you are my queen;
> For with my death the whole truth shall be seen.
> Your two great eyes will slay me suddenly;
> Their beauty shakes me who was once serene;
> Straight through my heart the wound is quick and keen.
> (*Rondel of Merciless Beauty*, Geoffrey Chaucer)

roundel

(ROUN dull)

a verse form similar to the French **rondeau**; created by Algernon Charles Swinburne

contains three stanzas, with four lines, 3 lines, and 4 lines each, including a refrain following the third and the tenth line (the refrain mimics some or all of the first line and rhymes with the second line) with the rhyme scheme *abaR bab abaR*

not to be confused with the rondel

Example:

> A roundel is wrought as a ring or a starbright sphere,
> With craft of delight and with cunning of sound unsought,
> That the heart of the hearer may smile if to pleasure his ear
>   A roundel is wrought.
>
> Its jewel of music is carven of all or of aught -
> Love, laughter, or mourning--remembrance of rapture or fear -
> That fancy may fashion to hang in the ear of thought.
>
> As a bird's quick song runs round, and the hearts in us hear
> Pause answer to pause, and again the same strain caught,
> So moves the device whence, round as a pearl or tear,
>   A roundel is wrought.
> (*A Century of Roundels*, Algernon Charles Swinburne)

---

roundelay

(ROUN dih lay)

a dancing song with a refrain

---

scansion

(SCAN shun)

the analysis of poetic meter (**scanning**), typically using visual symbols denoting the accent of the syllable (**diacritical marks**)

unstressed syllables are indicated by the slightly curved diacritical mark (ă, ĕ, ĭ, ŏ, ŭ)

stressed syllables are indicated by the accent grave (á, é, í, ó, ú)

[*see also* prosody]

---

septet

(sep TET)

a stanza with seven lines

[*see also* rhyme royal]

---

sestet (SES tet)	a six-line stanza that follows the octave in a **Petrarchan** or **Miltonic sonnet** usually begins with a **turn** (volta) in the first line
sestina (sess TEE nah)	a lyric poem of six six-lined (usually unrhymed) stanzas followed by a tercet (for a total of 39 lines); from "sixth" (Italian) **Example:** "Sestina" (Dante)
Shakespearean sonnet	a fourteen line sonnet consisting of three quatrains with the rhyme scheme *abab cdcd efef*, followed by a couplet rhyming *gg* also referred to as an **English sonnet** **Example:** Let me not to the marriage of true minds Admit impediments. Love is not love Which alters when it alteration finds, Or bends with the remover to remove: O no! it is an ever-fixed mark That looks on tempests and is never shaken; It is the star to every wand'ring bark, Whose worth's unknown, although his heighth be taken. Love's not Time's fool, though rosy lips and cheeks Within his bending sickle's compass come; Love alters not with his brief hours and weeks, But bears it out even to the edge of doom: If this be error and upon me proved, I never writ, nor no man ever loved. ("Sonnet 116," Shakespeare)

shanty	a maritime work song with the purpose of establishing a rhythm for the coordination of shipboard activities
	also referred to as a **sea shanty** or **chantey**

Example:

> I'll sing you a song, a good song of the sea
> With a way, hey, blow the man down
> And trust that you'll join in the chorus with me
> Give me some time to blow the man down
> (Anonymous)

short measure	quatrain that has three stresses in the first, second, and fourth line and four stresses in the fourth line, usually with the rhyme scheme *abab*
	also referred to as **short meter**

Skeltonics	poems having short lines of verse with two or three stresses per line and an identical rhyme repeated over several consecutive lines
	attributed to the style of poetry used by the Middle English poet John Skelton

sonnet	a lyric poem, usually consisting of fourteen lines, that typically follows a conventional rhyme scheme; from "little song" (Italian)

Examples:

> Let me not to the marriage of true minds
> Admit impediments. Love is not love
> Which alters when it alteration finds,
> Or bends with the remover to remove:
> O no! it is an ever-fixed mark
> That looks on tempests and is never shaken;
> It is the star to every wandering bark,
> Whose worth's unknown, although his height be taken.
> Love's not Time's fool, though rosy lips and cheeks
> Within his bending sickle's compass come:
> Love alters not with his brief hours and weeks,
> But bears it out even to the edge of doom.
> If this be error and upon me proved,
> I never writ, nor no man ever loved.
> ("Sonnet 116," Shakespeare)

[*see also* Petrarchan sonnet, Shakespearean sonnet]

sonnet cycle	a series of sonnets written on a common theme, usually to a loved one

also referred to as a **sonnet sequence**

examples include Elizabeth Barrett Browning's *Sonnets from the Portuguese*, John Donne's *Holy Sonnets*, and Sir Philip Sidney's "Astrophel and Stella"

Spenserian sonnet	a fourteen line poem ending with a couplet and having the rhyme scheme ***abab bcbc cdcd ee***

created by the English poet Sir Edmund Spenser

also referred to as a **link sonnet**

Example:

> One day I wrote her name upon the strand,
> But came the waves and washed it away:
> Again I wrote it with a second hand,
> But came the tide, and made my pains his prey.
> Vain man, said she, that dost in vain assay
> A mortal thing so to immortalize!
> For I myself shall like to this decay,
> And eek my name be wiped out likewise.
> Not so (quoth I), let baser things devise
> To die in dust, but you shall live by fame:
> My verse your virtues rare shall eternize,
> And in the heavens write your glorious name;
>   Where, when as death shall all the world subdue,
>   Our love shall live, and later life renew.
> (Edmund Spenser)

Spenserian stanza	a stanza form invented by the English poet Sir Edmund Spenser that contains eight lines of iambic pentameter and a concluding line of iambic hexameter (alexandrine) with the rhyme scheme ***ababbcbcc***

Example:

> Forth came that auncient Lord and aged Queene,
> Arayd in antique robes downe to the ground,
> And sad habiliments right well beseene;
> A noble crew about them waited round
> Of sage and sober Peres, all gravely gownd;
> Whom farre before did march a goodly band
> Of tall young men, all hable armes to sownd,
> But now they laurell braunches bore in hand;
> Glad signe of victorie and peace in all their land.
> (*The Faerie Queene*, Edmund Spenser)

spondee (SPAHN dee)	a metrical foot in poetry that consists of two stressed syllables (as in *dáylíght* or *cárpoól*) the adjective form is **spondaic** (spahn DAY ik) **Example:** "**Roúgh wínds** dŏ sháke thĕ dárlĭng búds ŏf Máy," ("Sonnet 18," Shakespeare)
sprung rhythm	a term coined by poet Gerard Manley Hopkins to label the metrical scansion of the irregular rhythm particularly used in English folk poetry within this scansion, a foot may have from one to four syllables as opposed to the two or three in common rhythm
stanza	a group of lines in a poem usually sharing some common characteristic (e.g., rhyme scheme, length, meter, theme); set off from other groups by a blank line sometimes referred to as a **stave** in odes, the stanza is sometimes referred to as a **strophe**
stichic (STIK ik)	poetry written in successive lines of verse that have the same meter and length but is not divided into stanzas [*see also* verse paragraph]
systole (SISS tole ee)	the shortening of a syllable or vowel sound to accommodate meter or rhyme **Example:** "I would go to the mill / To fetch the grain for my next m**ea**l" [the **ee** sound is shortened to accommodate the rhyme of the shorter **ih** sound] [*see also* diastole]

tail rhyme

a line of verse that follows but does not rhyme with a preceding couplet or triplet but rather an earlier line

Example:

> His steed was all a dapple grey
> Whose gait was ambling, on the way,
> Full easily and round
> **In land.**
> Behold, my lords, here is a fit!
> If you'll have any more of it,
> You have but to **command**.
> (*Tale of Sir Thopas*, Chaucer)

tanka

(TAHN kuh)

an ancient Japanese poetic form having thirty one syllables—five syllables in lines one and three and seven syllables in lines two, four, and five

Example:

> What are they to me,
> Silver, or gold, or jewels?
> How could they ever
> Equal the greater treasure
> That is a child? They can not.
> (Okura)

tercet

(TURR sit)

a stanza composed of three lines of verse

also referred to as a **triplet**

terza rima

(turt suh REE mah)

a three-line stanza (tercet) with an interlocking rhyme scheme; that is, the final word of the second line of each tercet rhymes with the final words of the first and third lines of the succeeding tercet (***aba bcb cdc ded*** etc.)

Example:

> O wild West Wind, thou breath of Autumn's **being**,
> Thou, from whose unseen presence the leaves **dead**
> Are driven, like ghosts from an enchanter **fleeing**
>
> Yellow, and black, and pale, and hectic **red**.
> Pestilence-stricken multitudes: O **thou**,
> Who chariotest to their dark wintry **bed**...
> ("Ode to the West Wind," Percy Shelley)

tetrameter

(tet TRAM uh turr)

a line of verse consisting of four metrical feet

Example:

> Thăt níght yoŭr greát gŭns ŭnăwáres,
> Shook all our coffins as we lay
> And broke the chancel window-squares,
> We thought it was the Judgment-day
> ("Channel Firing," Thomas Hardy)

touchstone

a brief excerpt of a widely acclaimed poem used as a standard for comparison for other poetic works

trimeter

(TRIHM uh turr)

a line of verse containing three metrical feet

Example:

> "Óh tŏ bé ĭn Énglănd / Now that April's there. . . ."
> ("Home Thoughts, from Abroad," Robert Browning)

triolet

(tree uh LAY *or* TRAHY uh let)

an eight-line stanza with the rhyme scheme ***abaaabab*** and written in iambic tetrameter

triple meter

a metrical foot consisting of three beats of unstress or stress; an anapest (*ănăpést*) or dactyl (*tángĕrĭne*)

tristich

(TRISS tik)

a poem or stanza of three lines

[*see also* quatrain]

trochee

(TROH kay)

a metrical foot in poetry that consists of one stressed syllable followed by one unstressed syllable (as in *tróchĕe, líttlĕ*)

the adjective form is **trochaic** (troh KAY ik)

Example:

> "Dóublĕ, dóublĕ, tóil ănd tróublĕ," (*Macbeth*, IV.i, Shakespeare)

turn	a change in tone, mood, or focus in a poem, particularly in a sonnet (between the octave and sestet in a Petrarchan sonnet and starting with the final couplet in a Shakespearean sonnet)
	also referred to as a **volta**
ubi sunt (ooh bee SOONT)	a common motif in medieval Latin poetry that reminisces on those dead or gone and conveys a theme of the fleeting nature of life and beauty; from "where are" (Latin)
verse	a term that refers to poetry in general, an individual poem, or an individual line of poetry
verse paragraph	poetry written in continuous lines of verse that have irregular meter and length
	[*see also* stichic]
versification (vur sih fih KAY shun)	the theory of meter, sound, and structure of poetry
villanelle (vill uh NELL)	a verse form that incorporates two rhymes and typically consists of five tercets and a quatrain
	the first and third lines of the opening tercet recur alternately at the end of the other tercets and together as the last two lines of the quatrain; from "peasant" (French, Italian)
	Example: "Do Not Go Gentle into That Good Night" (Dylan Thomas)
virgule (VUR gyool)	the slant mark (/) used in the scansion of poetry to indicate the division of feet

weak ending　replacing a normally stressed syllable with an unstressed syllable at the end of a line of verse

[*see also* feminine ending]

wrenched accent　a stress on a syllable not normally stressed in conversational speech to accommodate poetic meter

a variation is the **recessive accent**, which is the placement of stress on the first syllable of a two-syllable word that usually has a stress on the last syllable; often marked with an accent mark

Example:

"Or I with grief and **éxtreme** age shall perish" (*Richard III*, IV.iv, Shakespeare)

act	one of the major divisions of a play; classic plays are often divided into five acts whereas most modern plays are divided into three

agon (AG ohn)	the conflict between the protagonist and the antagonist in ancient Greek drama, or the debate or contest between two characters in ancient Greek comedy [*see also* deuteragonist]

anagnorisis
 	
(ah nag NOHR uh sis)
	the turning point in a drama in which a character (usually the protagonist) discovers a truth and finally recognizes what is really going on
	
	usually combined with the play's **peripeteia**
	
	also referred to as **discovery** or **recognition**
	
	Examples:
	
	When Macbeth in the tragedy *Macbeth* (Shakespeare) realizes that the prophecies told to him by the weird sisters contained double meanings:
	    To doubt the equivocation of the fiend
	    That lies like truth. "Fear not, till Birnam wood
	    Do come to Dunsinane," and now a wood
	    Comes toward Dunsinane.
	    (*Macbeth*, V.v, Shakespeare)
	
	[*see also* epiphany]

aposiopesis

(ah poh sahy oh PEE sis)

a rhetorical figure in which a speaker abruptly stops speaking, either from an external distraction or from an overwhelming emotion; from "silence" (Greek)

aposiopesis is usually written in text with ellipses (...) or a dash (—)

Example:

HAMLET:	A murderer and a villain
	A slave that is not twentieth part the tithe
	Of your precedent lord; a vice of kings;
	A cut-purse of the empire and the rule,
	That from a shelf the precious diadem stole,
	And put it in his pocket!
QUEEN:	No more!
HAMLET:	**A king of shreds and patches, —**
	Enter Ghost
	Save me, and hover o'er me with your wings,
	You heavenly guards! What would your gracious figure?

(*Hamlet*, III.iv, Shakespeare)

aside

when an onstage character in a drama addresses the audience to reveal some inner thought or feeling that is presumably inaudible to any other characters onstage; asides are usually marked as *[Aside]* in the script of a drama

canticum

(KAN tih kuhm)

the sung part of a Latin drama

[*see also* diverbium]

catastasis

(kah TAS tuh sihs)

the moment preceding the catastrophe in a tragedy; the climax (the four elements of a tragedy: **protasis**—exposition; **epistasis**—rising action; **catastasis**—climax; **catastrophe**—resolution)

not to be confused with the rhetorical meaning of this term, which is the beginning part of a rhetorical delivery

Example:

In Shakespeare's tragedy *Macbeth*, the catastasis is the scene in which Macduff confronts Macbeth and reveals to him the meaning of the weird sisters' third prophecy:

MACBETH: I bear a charmed life, which must not yield,
To one of woman born

MACDUFF: Despair thy charm;
And let the angel whom thou hast served
Tell thee, Macduff was from his mother's womb
Untimely ripp'd

[*see also* anagnorisis, peripeteia]

catastrophe

(kah TAS troh fee)

the culmination of a tragedy's falling action, which follows the catastasis (climax); from "overturning" (Greek)

known as a dénouement in non-tragic dramas

(the four elements of a tragedy: **protasis**—exposition; **epistasis**—rising action; **catastasis**—climax; **catastrophe**—resolution)

Example:

In Shakespeare's tragedy *Macbeth*, the catastrophe is the last scene in which Malcolm reclaims his crown.

[*see also* anagnorisis, peripeteia]

catharsis

(kah THAR sis)

the emotionally draining effect a tragic drama has on its audience during and after the catastrophe; from "purgation" or "purification" (Greek)

chorus

in Greek drama, an ensemble who danced and sang as they interjected commentary on the characters and plot

deuteragonist

(doo turr OGG ih nist)

either the antagonist or the foil to the protagonist in a Greek drama

[*see also* agon]

dialogue

(DAHY uh log)

conversation between two or more characters

diverbium

(dahy VURR bee um)

the spoken dialogue in a Latin drama

[*see also* canticum]

drama

a narrative, usually one that is serious, intended to be performed by actors in front of an audience

dramatic convention

a widely accepted technique or device common to drama, such as soliloquies, asides, and the use of stock characters

dramatic poetry

a play written chiefly in verse form to be performed before an audience, or a poem that incorporates dramatic devices

dramatis personae

(DRAM uh tiss purr SOH nee)

refers collectively to the characters represented in a play; from "persons of the play" (Latin)

usually, the dramatis personae are listed at the beginning of the play's script

dramaturgy

(DRAM uh turr jee)

the underlying principles of dramatic composition and theater production

dumb show

a silent performance that precedes and mimics the scene that follows

Example:

> The play within a play, "The Murder of Gonzago," in Shakespeare's *Hamlet* (III.ii) features a dumb show.

eiron

(AHY ron)

a stock character in ancient Greek comedies who, though wise, pretends to be foolish or poor

contrasted by the **alazon**, who is boastful yet foolish

Example:

> In *The Odyssey* (Homer), the title character, Odysseus, dresses as a beggar (the eiron) to gain access to his palace; he is contrasted by Irus, the actual foolish beggar (the alazon), with whom Odysseus engages in a fight.

epilogue

(EPP ih log)

the concluding section of a work; also, the recitation by an actor of the concluding section of a play (in the form of a speech), often requesting the applause of the audience and kind reviews from critics

Example:

> Now my charms are all o'erthrown
> And what strength I have's mine own
> ....
> As you from crimes would pardon'd be,
> Let your indulgence set me free.
> (*The Tempest*, V.i, Shakespeare)

epistasis

(eh PIHS tuh sihs)

the point in a tragedy immediately preceding the catastasis; from "near intensification" (Greek)

(the four elements of a tragedy: **protasis**— exposition; **epistasis**— rising action; **catastasis**— climax; **catastrophe**— resolution)

Example:

> In Shakespeare's tragedy *Macbeth*, the epistasis occurs when Macbeth slays Young Siward as the rest of Malcolm's army enters Macbeth's castle.

[*see also* anagnorisis, peripeteia]

epode (EPP ode)	the third part of a Greek dramatic chorus, following the strophe and antistrophe also, the third part of a **Pindaric ode**, which consists of three-stanzas
exodos (EKS uh dos)	the final section of a Greek drama; follows the final episode or stasimon; includes the resolution; from "a way out" (Greek)
fourth wall	the imaginary wall that separates the actors from the audience but allows the audience to view the action in a play
Freytag's Pyramid (FRAHY tag)	the structure of a typical five-act play, which loosely corresponds with the five acts of a drama: consists of the following: **introduction, rising action, climax, falling action,** and **dénouement** (or, in the case of a tragedy, the **catastrophe**)
hamartia (hah mar TEE uh)	the mistake or misunderstanding that leads the protagonist in a tragedy to his or her downfall; from "error" or "failure" (Greek) [*see also* tragic flaw]
hubris (HYOO briss)	refers to the arrogance of the protagonist in a Greek tragedy in which he or she defies the gods; from "insolence" (Greek) also referred to as **hybris** (HAHY briss) [*see also* hamartia, sophrosyne, tragic flaw]
interlude (INN turr lood)	a short play or other form of entertainment performed between acts in a play; from "between play" (Latin)

machinery	a device that raised or lowered a supernatural figure onto the stage in classic drama
	also refers to any supernatural figure featured in a dramatic work or epic poem
	[*see also* deus ex machina]

melodrama (MELL oh drah mah)	an overly sentimental work with exaggerated characters and contrived plot situations; from "song act" (Greek)

Middle Comedy	a type of Greek comedy popular in the 4th century BCE featuring mild satire of literary and philosophical themes
	the chorus takes no part in this form, unlike Old Comedy in which the chorus is prominent
	the most prominent playwright of this form was Aristophanes
	[*see also* Old Comedy, New Comedy]

mise en scène (meez en SEN)	the staging (prop/actor placement, costumes, lighting) of a dramatic production

monologue (MAHN uh log)	an extended speech spoken by one character (either alone or to other characters)
	Example: the "Alas, poor Yorick" speech spoken by Hamlet to his friend Horatio (*Hamlet*, V.i, Shakespeare)
	[*see also* soliloquy]

monopolylogue (mahn uh POL ih log)	a play in which the same performer plays several parts or characters (often used in monodramas)

nemesis (NIM ih sis)	the manifestation of the gods' retribution for crimes and insults, particularly hubris
New Comedy	a type of Greek comedy popular in the 3rd century BCE featuring stereotypical characters and contrived plots concerning love and intergenerational conflict the chorus took no part in this form, unlike Old Comedy in which the chorus was prominent the most prominent playwright of this form was Menander [*see also* Old Comedy, Middle Comedy]
one-act play	a short one-act play that has continuous action, sparse props, and few characters; usually lasts from ten minutes to under an hour **Examples:** *The Zoo Story* (Edward Albee) *Mountain Language* (Harold Pinter) *Salomé* (Oscar Wilde)
obligatory scene (oh BLIG uh tohr ee SEEN)	a scene that must be shown, either as a convention of the genre or because it is expected by the audience also referred to as a **scène à faire** examples include a confrontation between the protagonist and the antagonist or the use of futuristic technology in a science fiction production
Old Comedy	a type of Greek comedy popular in the 5th century BCE featuring political satire and obscene, scatological elements the chorus takes an active part in this form, unlike New Comedy in which the chorus is absent the most prominent playwright of this form was Aristophanes [*see also* Middle Comedy, New Comedy]

pantomime

(PAN toh mime)

play acting using no words and only physical gestures

also referred to as **mime**

[*see also* dumb show]

parabasis

(puh RAB uh sis)

the resolution or epilogue of an ancient Greek play

consisted of a choral ode, which served to express the playwright's stated purpose or moral for the play

parados

(pair oh DOSE)

a song sung by a Greek chorus as it first entered the theater, or where the chorus and actors made their entrances from either side into the orchestra

periaktos

(pare ee AK tohs)

a 3-sided revolving set used in ancient Greek dramas

peripeteia

(pair uh puh TEE uh *or* pair uh puh TAHY uh)

in a tragedy, a drastic turn for the worse in a character's circumstances, ultimately leading to his or her tragic fall

in a comedy, when previously lost fortunes are restored to the protagonist

also referred to as **peripety** (puh RIP ih tee); from "sudden change" (Greek)

playwright

the author of a play

prologue

an introductory statement preceding a literary work; in a Greek tragedy, the opening section of a play, preceding the first choral ode

also referred to as **prologos**

props

the materials that the actors of a theater production use in the staging of a play

[*see also* set, staging]

proskenion (proh SKEE nee on)	the elevated platform (stage) in front of the skene; used to separate the actors in a tragedy from the chorus
protasis (PROT uh sihs)	the exposition of a drama; when the characters, setting, and plot are introduced followed by the epistasis and catastrophe; from "stretching forward" (Greek) (the four elements of a tragedy: **protasis**—exposition; **epistasis**—rising action; **catastasis**—climax; **catastrophe**—resolution) [*see also* anagnorisis, peripeteia]
Satyr play (SAY turr *or* SAT urr)	an ancient Greek drama that good-naturedly mocked myths and legends; a parody or farce in Greek drama that often featured low, common diction and sexual innuendoes
scene	a section in a drama in which there is a specific focus and, usually, no shift in setting
Scottish play, that	a term used to refer to any production of William Shakespeare's *Macbeth* due to superstitions suggesting bad luck when performing the play
screenplay	the script for a movie, including camera and stage directions, scenery, and dialogue
script	the manuscript that details the stage directions and dialogue of a drama; from "written" (Latin)
set	the collection of props and staging materials that establish a scene in a play

skene

(SKEE nee)

in Ancient Greek drama, the background building in front of the orchestra from which the actors emerged; this is also where props and costumes were stored

the skene was common in ancient Greek performances and is the basis for the modern term *scene*

---

skit

a short, comical satiric performance

[*see also* sketch]

---

soliloquy

(so LIL oh kwee)

a speech in which a solitary character, expressing private thoughts and feelings, presumably speaks to himself or herself; a type of monologue

Example:

Hamlet's "To be or not to be" speech (*Hamlet*, III.i, Shakespeare)

---

sophrosyne

(suh FROSS uh nee)

careful, deliberative action on the part of the protagonist; from "prudent" (Greek)

contrast with **hubris**

---

stage directions

instructions to actors onstage as what to do before, during, and after delivering their respective lines

---

staging

the selection and placement of props and actors for a drama

[*see also* set]

---

stasimon

(STAS uh mon)

the section of a tragedy that follows each episode; the **stasima** (plural of *stasimon*) of a tragedy include dancing and singing by the chorus

stichomythia (stik oh MITH ee uh)	dialogue in drama in which two characters answer each other in alternating single or half lines, with one character's replies partially incorporating what the other character has just said; from "a line of speech" (Greek) **Example:** HAMLET: Now, mother, what's the matter? QUEEN: Hamlet, thou hast thy father much offended. HAMLET: Mother, you have my father much offended. QUEEN: Come, come, you answer with an idle tongue HAMLET: Go, go, you question with a wicked tongue (*Hamlet*, III.iv, Shakespeare)
strophe (STROFE)	the first part of a choral ode that precedes the antistrophe in a Greek tragedy; from "turning" (Greek) also refers to a stanza, especially in an ode, or a verse paragraph in free verse poetry
theater in the round	a presentation in which the stage is surrounded on all sides by the audience
thespian (THESS pee un)	related to a dramatic performance, particularly in reference to acting
tragic flaw	a character trait in a tragic hero or heroine that brings about his or her downfall; a tragic flaw is a type of hamartia **hubris** is a common tragic flaw **Example:** Hamlet's tragic flaw could be his inability to act, which ultimately creates an opportunity for Claudius (the king) to plot his death. (*Hamlet*, Shakespeare)
tragic hero	a character who has the potential for greatness but also possesses a tragic flaw, which ultimately leads to his downfall [*see also* hamartia, hubris]

treatment	a sketch of a film or television production that lays out the preliminary elements of the script
two-hander	a dramatic presentation with only two main characters or speaking parts
the Unities	fundamentals of neoclassical drama inspired by Aristotle's *Poetics*, consisting of • **unity of time** (single, continuous time of setting) • **unity of action** (no subplots) • **unity of place** (a single setting)
well-made play	a negative term for a play that is functional but not necessarily enjoyable or critically accepted

abridged	a term used to describe a condensed version of a text, one that retains the essential aspects of the text yet omits other less suitable or less important parts
annotation (ann oh TAY shun)	supplementary notes in a text, usually for clarification or elaboration
bibliography (bib lee OGG ruh fee)	a list of resources consulted or referenced in a work; differs from a works cited page in that a bibliography lists all resources consulted in the compilation of a work rather than just those cited in the work
blog	a continuous journal of news or human interest stories published on the Internet; a portmanteau of "web log"
broadside	a one-sided sheet of printed material (news, advertisements, songs) distributed to the public also referred to as a **broadsheet**
caption (CAP shun)	a descriptive note attached to a picture, table, or diagram
circular	an advertisement or statement of public notice distributed to the general public
codex (KO deks)	an ancient manuscript, particularly fragments of the Holy Bible; from "from wooden tablets" (Latin) the plural of codex is **codices** (KAH duh sees) [*see also* index]

codicil (KAHD uh sull)	an appendix or supplement to a text
colophon (KAHL uh fone)	a publisher's logo on the title page, or a page that lists publishing details of the text
concordance (kun KORD ants)	an alphabetized listing of main terms and their location(s) in a text
copy	the body text used in a periodical and usually preceded by a **headline**
copy-text	the particular manuscript used for a published work
diagram	a visual representation of a process, analysis, or a mathematical problem
duodecimo (doo oh DESS ih moh)	a manuscript size resulting from folding a sheet of printer's paper twelve times, resulting in 24 pages also referred to as a **twelvemo**
edition	a particular printing in a series of printings, or one version of a multi-version work [*see also* issue]
emendation (em en DAY shun)	a correction to an edition of a text based on the belief that an earlier edition had been transcribed incorrectly from the original manuscript
epigraph (EPP uh graff)	a motto or quotation at the beginning of a novel that sets forth the theme

erasure

(ee RAY shurr)

the practice of visibly marking out a term, so that the reader is aware that the term has been deleted

Example:

"The men ~~and their families~~ were sent to the battlefield shortly before dawn."

errata

(eh RAT uh)

a list of errors in a published text; usually provided as a supplement after publishing

folio

(FOH lee oh)

a book that results from printer paper being folded down one time, resulting in four pages per sheet; from "in a leaf, sheet" (Latin)

results in a book that is roughly fifteen inches tall

font

the size and visual style of printed text

glossary

(GLOSS uh ree)

a list of key terms and their respective definitions in a text; from "foreign word" (Greek)

graph

a visual representation of data, relationships, or sequences

holograph

an original manuscript written completely by the author

hypertext

a link in a document (particularly a web page on the Internet) that connects to another part of the document or another document entirely

also referred to as a **hyperlink**

index (IN deks)	a comprehensive list of terms, related figures, and cross-references in a text and their location(s) in a text; from "pointer" (Latin) the plural of index is **indices** (IN duh sees) [*see also* concordance]
issue	a particular printing of a periodical [*see also* edition]
lacuna (lah KEW nah)	a missing part of a manuscript or text
leaf	a single sheet of manuscript of two printed or blank pages, one on each side
leaflet	a small sheet of paper, containing printed information, folded into leaves (two pages) and usually distributed to the public at no cost
lexicon (LEKS ih kahn)	a dictionary another form of this term, **lexis**, refers to the complete vocabulary of a language
libretto (lih BRET oh)	the text of an opera or other vocal performance in bound form; from "booklet" (Italian)
manuscript (MAN yoo skript)	literally, a hand-written draft of a document; also refers to any unpublished work meant for eventual publication; from "book written by hand" (Latin)
monograph (MAHN oh graff)	an essay or book written on a single subject; from "single writing" (Greek)

octavo (okk TAHV oh)	a book that results from printer paper being folded down four times, resulting in sixteen pages per sheet (eight sheets total); from "eighth the size" (Latin) results in a book that is roughly five to six by eight to nine and a half inches
palimpsest (PAL imp sest)	a used manuscript which has been written over due to the fading of the original text; from "scraped again" (Greek)
pamphlet (PAM flit)	a manuscript loosely stitched or stapled together with a paper cover; often used to convey the author's beliefs on a subject [*see also* manifesto, tract, treatise]
passage (PASS ij)	an excerpt of a text
passus (PASS us)	a section or division of a literary work, such as a chapter, stanza, or canto
preface (PREF ihs)	an introduction, usually written by the author, to a book that outlines its scope and subject matter
pulled quote	a selection of text that is extracted and presented in a distinct manner (usually a larger typeface) to draw attention to the excerpt
quarto (KWORE toh)	a book that results from printer paper being folded down two times, resulting in eight pages per sheet (four sheets total); from "fourth the size" (Latin) results in a book that is roughly nine and a half by twelve inches

recension

(ree SIN shun)

a version of a literary work derived through textual criticism and revisions of other versions of the work

recto

(REK toh)

the right-hand side of a printed book (odd-numbered pages); from "right hand of the page" (Latin)

redaction

(ree DAK shun)

the revision and proofreading of a manuscript

revision

a manuscript that has been modified into a new version; a stage of the writing process in which a draft is modified

sidebar

a distinct part of a printed page that is formatted differently yet serves to supplement the main text

text

the words in a written work, or a general term for a literary work

tract

a treatise or manifesto distributed to the public in pamphlet form

typography

the art and practice of typesetting, printing, and arrangement of words

[*see also* concrete poetry, font]

unabridged

the complete version of a text, with no omissions or shortening

verso

(VURR soh)

generally, the left-hand side of a printed book (even-numbered pages); often referred to as the page that is opposite to the title page in a text and includes edition and copyright information; from "turned page" (Latin)

volume	any text bound as a book, or a collection of related texts
watermark	a semi-transparent background text or image that is printed on a page

Abbreviations and Symbols

ampersand	the symbol for the word *and* (&)
BCE	before current era (contemporary version of the time designation BC)
ca.	about, approximately; from "circa" (Latin)
CE	current era (contemporary version of the time designation AD)
cf.	see also (as a cross-reference); from "confer" (Latin)
circumflex (SUR kum fleks)	an accent mark (â, ê, î, ô, û) used in some languages to indicate that the vowel or syllable is pronounced in a particular way
e.g.	for example; from "exempli gratia" (Latin)
emoticon (ee MOTE ih kahn)	keyboard characters that have been combined to represent sideway images; often used in electronic communication (e.g., chats, email, text messages) examples include the smiley face **:)** and the winking face **;)**
et al.	and others; from "et alli" (Latin)
etc.	and so on; from "et cetera" (Latin)
ibid.	in the same place; from "ibidem" (Latin)
op. cit.	in the work previously cited; from "opus citatum" (Latin)
p.	page
pp.	pages
pilcrow (PILL kroh)	the symbol for a paragraph; also referred to as a **paragraph mark** (¶)
RE:	in the matter of, concerning; from "res" (Latin)

sic.	the preceding word or phrase contains an error, but it is being quoted exactly from the source; from "thus; so" (Latin)
tittle (TIT ull)	the part of the letter *i* that is a dot
umlaut (OOM lout)	the two dots used as a diacritic over vowels in some languages, often to indicate a different punctuation from the vowel without the mark (ä, ë, ï, ö, ü)
viz.	namely or that is; from "videlicet" (Latin)

Index of Authors, Poets, and Critics

Index of Titles

Index of Terms

identical rhyme, *218*, 256

ideogram, *98*

idiolect, *183*

idiom, *85*, 146, 178

idyll, *24*

ignoratio elenchi, *124*

illocutionary act, *138*

imagery, 15, 52, 59, 119, *183*, 185, 195, 211, 238

Imagism, *51*, 55, 60

imperative sentence, 158

implied metaphor, *85*, 89

implied reader, *69*

Impressionistic criticism, *69*

in medias res, 18, *183*

In Memoriam stanza, *241*

incluing, 20, *184*, 210

incremental repetition, *242*

independent clause, 146, 147, 150, *152*, 154, 157, 158

indeterminacy, 65, *69*

index, 279, *282*

indignatio, *125*, 130

indirect characterization, *168*

induction, 114, *125*

inflection, *216*, 221

ingénue, 169, *184*, 206

initial rhyme, *213*

innuendo, *125*, 126

inopinatum, *125*

inscape/instress, *184*

intentional fallacy, *69*, 72

interior monologue, *207*

interlude, 9, 42, *270*

internal conflict, 177, *198*

internal monologue, *207*

internal rhyme, 214, *216*, 218

internally focalized, *179*

interpolation, *69*

interpretation, 9, 63, 66, 68, *69*, 73, 75, 76

interrogative sentence, *158*

intertextuality, 64, *70*

intimation, 125, *126*

intonation, *216*

intrusive narrator, *199*

invective, 33, *126*

inversion, *144*, 159

inverted syntax, *152*

invocation, *184*

ipse dixit, *126*

irony, 23, 79, *86*, *87*

isocolon, 123, *152*

issue, 280, *282*

Italian sonnet, *249*

J

Jacobean Age, 48, *51*

jangle, *214*

jargon, 174, *184*

jeremiad, *185*

jeu d'esprit, 177, *185*

jeu de mots, *92*

jingle, *242*

jingoism, *126*, 212

jongleur, *185*

jumped the shark, *185*

Jungian criticism, *70*, 71, 74

Juvenalian satire, *37*

juvenile fiction, *25*

juvenilia, *25*

juxtaposition, *153*

K

kabuki, *25*

kairos, 109, 121, *126*, 127, 132, 137

kenning, *243*

King's English, the, *185*

kitchen-sink drama, *25*

kitsch, *200*

Künstlerroman, 11, *25*

L

Lacanian criticism, *70*, 73, 74

lacuna, *282*

lai, *243*

laisse, *12*

Lake Poets, *51*

lament, *16*

lamentation, 14, *16*, 41, 185

lampoon, *37*

language, 13, 15, 47, 55, 64, 66, 67, 68, *70*, 71, 75, 76, 85, 97, 98, 99, 111, 112, 126, 127, 137, 146, 150, 161, 170, 174, 180, 182, 183, 184, *185*, 193, 200, 203, 205, 207, 211, 221, 244, 250, 282

langue, *70*

Latinate, *186*

leaf, *282*

leaflet, *282*

legend, 21, *25*, 27, 36, 65, 73, 85, 127, 212

legendarium, *186*

leitmotif, 71, 165, 183, *186*, 190

leonine rhyme, *216*

leptologia, *127*

level stress, *243*

lexicon, *282*

lexis, *282*

libretto, 31, *282*

light ending, *236*

light rhyme, *216*

light verse, 214, *243*

ligne donnée, 222, *243*

limerick, 243, *244*

limited point of view, *199*

lingo, *186*

References

For further elaboration, the following sources may be useful.

Abrams, M.H. *A Glossary of Literary Terms*. New York: HB College Publishers, 1999. Print.

Baldick, Chris. *Oxford Concise Dictionary of Literary Terms*. 2nd edition. Oxford: Oxford University Press, 2001. Print.

Beckson, Karl and Arthur Ganz. *Literary Terms: A Dictionary*. 3rd ed. New York: Noonday Press, 1989. Print.

Burton, Gideon. *Silvae Rhetoricae: The Forest of Rhetoric*. 10 July 2003. Web.

Cuddon, J.A. *Dictionary of Literary Terms & Literary Theory*. Ed. C.E. Preston. 3rd Edition. London: Penguin, 1998. Print.

Cummings, Michael. *Literary Terms (Including Figures of Speech)*. 4 August 2006. Web.

Eidenmuller, Michael E. *American Rhetoric*. 2001. n.d. Web.

Lanham, Richard A. *A Handlist of Rhetorical Terms*. 2nd Edition. Berkeley: University of California Press, 1991. Print.

Makaryk, Irene Rima. *Encyclopedia of Contemporary Literary Theory*. Toronto: University of Toronto Press, 2000. Print.

Murfin, Ross and Supryia M Ray. *The Bedford Glossary of Critical and Literary Terms*. 2nd edition. Boston: Bedford/St. Martin's, 2003. Print.

Prince, Gerald. *Dictionary of Narratology*. Lincoln: University of Nebraska Press, 2003. Print.

Made in the USA
San Bernardino, CA
07 September 2014